THE STORY OF ISRAEL

From Joshua to Alexander the Great

WESTMINSTER GUIDES TO THE BIBLE

Edwin M. Good, General Editor

THE STORY
OF
ISRAEL

From Joshua to Alexander the Great

by
STEPHEN SZIKSZAI

Philadelphia
THE WESTMINSTER PRESS

PRINTED IN THE UNITED STATES OF AMERICA

Contents

Preface

To MODERN Americans, history often seems like a lot of past without much significance. To the ancient Hebrew, who had no word for "history," what the word signifies was the most vital and exciting factor in his life. Indeed, it may be argued that the Hebrew's sense of the past was what made the future so important to him. For the Hebrew knew the past not simply as a list of dates and battles — dates he could not have cared less about, though he could muster some interest in battles. Rather, he knew history from the inside; knew it as something that happened to him because it happened to his ancestors.

And it is the sensation of participating in a story of profound importance, because it happened to our spiritual ancestors, that makes the reading of this book such an adventure. Dates there are, but they are the important ones, the ones memorable because of the pivotal events they contained. And battles there are, and kings, high priests, emperors, and prime ministers. History is always full of those. Yet this history does not forget the little man, the man who we would be if we had been there. There is a sense in this book of history from the inside, history as the Hebrew himself knew it, that history is full not only of kings and emperors but of God. For, as Professor Szikszai takes pains to make clear, whatever else history

7

might consist of, for the Hebrew what was important was the continuing action of God. And when God takes center stage, the relative greatnesses of great men and of small men fall into shadow. Here lies the fascination of the story of Israel.

The Westminster Guides to the Bible grew in the first instance out of the stimulus of the Layman's Theological Library. If, we thought, laymen in the church could be so eloquently encouraged to be theologians, why could they not be encouraged to be Biblical scholars as well? In the modern resurgence of serious thinking about the Christian faith, Bible study has played a major role. But the methods and results of this recent study have not been made available to laymen.

The Westminster Guides to the Bible seek to fill this gap. In nine brief volumes, we introduce the riches of the major portions of the Bible and of the period " between the Testaments." The writers share the conviction that the Bible lies at the heart of Christianity, and that it is imperative that laymen be aided to take a firm grip on Biblical faith. We are certain that this means no denial of the mind. On the contrary, the Bible demands the utmost our minds can give it, and searching study repays our efforts with new insights.

Of course, we are primarily concerned with the Bible, not with our books about it. We hope that the reader will have his Bible in hand as he reads these books, and will turn to it again when he has finished. We dare to hope that he will turn from these guides to the Bible itself with greater anticipation.

And it is with laymen, who are the backbone of the church, that we are concerned. We have written, not for scholars already learned, but for those who seek to learn. We are certain that no wishy-washy faith, no cheap " religiousness," is wanted. In the vigor of Biblical faith we trust that the reader will find invigoration. If so, the church of Christ will be served.

Edwin M. Good

CHAPTER I | *A Past with a Point*

I F A person wanted to tell the story of his life, he would not relate every little thing that had happened to him since his birth. Rather, he would tell about the important things: his parents, the schools where he studied, his wife and children, the jobs he has held, and the interests and hobbies he has.

Similarly, even the most detailed history of a nation would hasten through the humdrum years and concentrate on the crucial events, the religious and cultural trends of an era, and the influence of great men and women. This short account of Israel cannot paint every detail, but will sketch only the great events and trends in the life of the Old Testament people.

In retelling the story of Israel, we will rely upon written and archaeological evidence. We will consult all the books of the Old Testament, but especially the history books. There we see the story through Israel's own eyes. But other eyes also looked at some parts of the story; the records of Egypt, Assyria, Babylon, and Persia occasionally have something important to say about Israel. Yet we know more about Israel than the written records reveal. Archaeologists have excavated many remains that, though they cannot be read like a book, help to fill the blank places in the picture of the life of Israel.

The story of Israel is a story of aspirations, intrigues, politics, and wars. But above all, it is the story of faith, for it cannot be separated from the faith by which Israel proclaimed that God is the sovereign ruler of mankind's history, and that he chose Israel to be his light for the nations.

THE HISTORICAL BOOKS OF THE BIBLE

All the books of the Old Testament contribute some fact, color, thought, or insight to the story of Israel. But two major historical works in the Old Testament present the story of Israel itself, the so-called "Deuteronomic history" and the Chronicler's history.

The Deuteronomic history consists of the books of Deuteronomy, Joshua, Judges, Samuel, and Kings. The unknown author or authors probably wrote shortly before the death of King Josiah of Judah (609 B.C.). In writing his work the Deuteronomic author utilized ancient written traditions of the people, court annals, chronicles dealing with the deeds of the kings, documents from the archives of the Jerusalem Temple, and traditions that were still being orally transmitted. An editor or editors completed the work during the Babylonian exile (about 550 B.C.) by contributing, among other details, an account of the fall of Jerusalem and the deportation of its inhabitants into exile. Storing such a vast treasury of information, the Deuteronomic historical work supplies most of the reliable data concerning the story of the people from the time of the conquest of Canaan to the Babylonian captivity.

The other historical work is that of the Chronicler, which includes the books of Chronicles, Ezra, and Nehemiah. The Chronicler wrote shortly before the end of the fourth century B.C. and brought the story of Israel approximately up to that date. For events before the Babylonian exile, he quoted extensively from the books of Samuel and Kings. The Chronicler considered the Southern Kingdom, Judah, as the sole legitimate representative of the "people of Israel"; therefore his work shows no interest in the fate of the Northern Kingdom. In spite of this limitation, the books of Chronicles contain some valuable additional information even for the time before exile. The significance of the Chronicler's history, however, reaches its highest peak when it concerns the period of restoration after the Babylonian exile and most notably for the times of Nehemiah and Ezra. The Chronicler included in his work some original documents of the Temple archives, correspondence, royal edicts, genealogical tables, lists of Temple personnel, and the memoirs of Nehemiah and Ezra.

Though the works of the Deuteronomic writer and the Chronicler are called "history" books, they are historical works only in a special sense of the word. These books were not written merely for the sake of preserving the past to satisfy the thirst for knowledge or the curiosity of the reader. Unlike modern writers of history, the Biblical historians were not concerned with critical evaluation of the sources they used. They did not present objective studies in the history of Israel, though they unrelentingly pursued the truth with sober realism, neither beautifying nor erasing the memories of the evil deeds of such great men and admired heroes as David and Solomon. The purpose of the authors was neither to glorify the nation nor to indulge in the sheer joy of storytelling.

These Biblical writers did not look at Israel's history indifferently, as unconcerned spectators. They belonged to the people of Israel and personally shared in its memories and expectations. They might therefore be compared with preachers who looked back over the whole span of Israel's existence and who documented with the events of Israel's history their conviction that Israel owed loyalty to God, who was the Lord of history. Like sermons, the historical books tried to persuade their contemporaries that the road to hope leads through repentance for the sins of the past of Israel and in a renewed total allegiance to the Lord.

REDEMPTIVE HISTORY AND THE CHOSEN PEOPLE

The Biblical writers of history testified to their belief that God is the Lord of history. They knew that all changes in human society, regardless of their specific economic, political, social, or cultural character, were subject to God's will. History, the chain of events, is not a mere human affair formed and forged in the interplay, action, and reaction of human and natural forces. There is an element in human history that transcends the analysis of political, economical, or any other components. This element is God's will; God actively takes part in the formation of history and he reveals his plan for man through history.

The conviction that God is the Lord of history should not be taken to mean that God is working incessantly as one force among the other forces within human history. The Lordship of God over history does not mean either that he allies himself with the godly nations against the godless ones or that he continually hands out rewards and punishments. That the Lord is the Lord of history signifies that he gives purpose and goal to history and that he can intervene at his pleasure any time. At *decisive* moments the Lord breaks through the flux of history and gives new impetus to the unfolding of mankind's destiny. The Lord is not a part of history or merely a force within history. The faith of the Biblical writers told them that the Lord is absolute sovereign over the world and mankind, and that no human being can resist the Ruler of the world.

Biblical faith is aware that the stream of events in all its complexity, embracing the whole of the human sphere, is under God's hand and will, and accordingly it is not a mass of unrelated events haphazardly thrown together. Biblical faith also denies that history is a treadmill, where events of the past aimlessly reoccur. History is not a meaningless maze of blind alleys and dead-end streets, but a highway that leads somewhere. Though we cannot see what is beyond the next bend of the road, we know there is a goal. No human agents have devised, planned, and agreed upon this goal, but God himself has set the goal of history. In his inexplicable mercy, God wants to bring salvation to mankind through history. Estranged from God, from his fellow men, and from himself, man needs reconciliation, that is, a deliverance from the sin that is the source of rebellion, hatred, anxiety, and the whole human misery. The interlocking events of history lead, according to the grand plan of God, to the redemption of mankind. Thus history, Biblical faith asserts, is redemptive history.

In the design of redemptive history, God allotted a unique place to ancient Israel. God chose Israel as his very own possession. The election of Israel took place first in Abraham the patriarch, whom God called out from the heathen world to be the forefather of the nation Israel and to become through her a blessing for all nations of the world. (Gen. 12:1-3.) This election God sealed with the covenant of Sinai, in which the people of Israel became to him a " kingdom of priests and a holy nation " (Ex. 19:6). Election implied a privilege, but more than that, it was a duty and increased responsibility. Israel was entrusted by God with a missionary responsibility of worldwide dimensions so that she might become a light for all the nations. The divine plan of history envisions the redemption of mankind, and Israel's duty was to serve God's purpose in the world. If Israel failed to follow the Lord, God used other nations as rods of chastisement against Israel.

When, despite the divine urging and warning, Israel had not fulfilled her mission, God sent his Son to redeem mankind from sin, anxiety, and futility. And God made the church, the community of those who accept Christ as their Lord and Savior, the heir to the divine election and the missionary obligation that Israel had failed. In continuation of Israel's mission, the church, as the servant of the Lord, proclaims the good news of the salvation wrought in Christ to all the nations. This explains why the history of ancient Israel is meaningful and important for modern Christians. The Christian church, being the heir of Israel, cannot be indifferent to the history of the chosen people.

Inevitably, questions come to mind: Why did Israel become God's chosen people? Why did she receive the distinction of her mission? To answer that the Hebrews possessed a religious genius comparable to the genius of the Greeks for the arts and philosophy and to that of the Romans for law and government would be blatant disregard of the Biblical witness. For Israel also explored the mystery of divine decision. But the only answer she found was a new mystery. The sovereign Ruler of mankind chose Israel from among the nations of the world, not because of her excellence, but because he, inexplicably, loved her (see Deut. 7:6-8; 9:6; 10:14-15).

The story of Israel in this book starts at the time of Joshua and ends with the era of Alexander the Great. These are arbitrary limits. The beginnings of Israel's story reach back to Abraham, and the other end includes at least the coming of Jesus Christ. Yet the invasion under Joshua's leadership is a good beginning, for through the conquest of Canaan the descendants of Abraham received the land promised to their ancestor, and that was the stage where the drama of Israel's national life could unfold. Similarly, Alexander the Great's conquest of the East at the end of the fourth century B.C. brought into the life of Israel a new element that cannot be underestimated. For in Alexander's time the Greek culture and Israel's faith met face to face. As a result, the church, the

New Israel, later had at her disposal an international language, Greek, in which the first Christian missionaries could proclaim their faith to the world.

The story of Israel is woven from the lives, thoughts, and struggles of the men and women of the people of Israel. Heroes and cowards, kings and rebels, saints and idolators, marched together with prophets, priests, and psalmists in a majestic procession and prepared the road, yearningly or unwittingly, for the advent of the Child who was " set for the fall and rising of many in Israel " (Luke 2:34).

CHAPTER 2 | *Conquest of the Promised Land*

THE world of the Old Testament represents a small part of the world as known in modern times. Asia Minor, the so-called " Fertile Crescent " that curves from Mesopotamia to the southeast coast of the Mediterranean Sea, and Egypt were the scenes where the drama of Biblical history took place. The Greek islands with Crete and Cyprus, the Iranian high plateau, the great Arabian desert, and the land of Ethiopia formed the outermost frontiers of the world of Biblical times. This world, though small, contributed many achievements to human culture. Here human society evolved from small agricultural settlements to city-states and great empires.

Agriculture, the domestication of animals, and skill in perfecting tools and household articles prepared the way for the artistic construction of palaces and temples, for painting, sculpture, and writing. The invention of writing gave wings to human spirit. Inscriptions covered monuments and walls of palaces, temples, and tombs. Annals of royal courts, laws and legal decisions, business contracts and private letters, myths and legends, hymns and rituals, found their way to written expression. In Mesopotamia the scribes wrote on clay tablets with cuneiform (wedge-shaped) signs; these characters served first as pictures of objects and later as signs for the syllables of

16

words. In Egypt the highly decorative hieroglyphs also represented picture writing at first, but later they, too, developed into a nearly alphabetic script. The modern English alphabet can trace its family tree through Latin and Greek scripts to the ancient Near East, notably to the Phoenician script, the first easily manageable alphabet of some twenty-two letters. Indeed, the ancient Near East was a fascinating world where human life encountered the great adventure of civilization.

THE PROMISED LAND

The Promised Land itself occupied the point of balance in this small but highly dynamic world. A glance at the map will show that most of the major routes on land and sea met in the territory of Palestine, the Biblical "land of Canaan." Caravans from east, north, and south crossed through the land. Because of its central position, Canaan served not merely as a meeting ground of commerce but also as a battleground for competing empires, civilizations, and religions. The rival empires of Mesopotamia and Egypt vied with each other and with the land-hungry nomads of the Arabian desert for possession of this strip of fertile land.

The Canaanites (who are sometimes called "Amorites" in the Old Testament) were the original inhabitants of the land. They did not establish national unity, although they had a common language, religion, and civilization. The jealousy and conflicting interests of the self-asserting military aristocracies and selfish petty kings of the city-states of Canaan kept the land in constant hopeless division. Walled cities, such as Jerusalem, Hebron, Megiddo, and Bethel, were independent city-states, and their jurisdiction extended over the surrounding villages, which provided food for the cities and expected military protection in return. These petty states repeatedly formed alliances and conducted wars against one another. In spite of this division in the land, throughout the larger part of the second millennium B.C., the Canaanite cities acknowledged, at least theoretically, the overlordship of Egypt. The increase or decline of the Egyptian influence upon Canaan depended on the power of the changing Pharaohs who tried to wield the scepter over both Egypt and the provinces. Energetic Egyptian monarchs stationed strong garrisons in Palestine and wrested heavy tributes from the Canaanite petty kings, but when a weak Pharaoh occupied the throne the scene in the province of Canaan often turned into chaos.

The situation that existed in Canaan during the years from 1400 to 1360 B.C. was repeated again and again. This particular period is well known, thanks to the so-called " Amarna Letters," a collection of documents from the royal archives of Amenhotep IV, excavated at modern Tell el-Amarna in Egypt. In these letters to the Pharaoh, the rival princes of Canaan accused one another of duplicity, conspiracy, and outright treason. They eloquently asserted their own innocence and asked for the military intervention of the Egyptian king against their own Canaanite rivals. Besides these " family " quarrels, the Amarna Letters report the menacing inroads of a nomadic group, the Habiru. Some scholars assume that the Habiru were identical with the Biblical Hebrews, but this theory is very questionable. The Habiru had been threatening the Near Eastern cities throughout the whole Fertile Crescent between the nineteenth and twelfth centuries B.C., but the Biblical account gives no indication of such long and widespread influence of the Hebrews. Besides, the name " Habiru " is not the name of a people but of a *class* of people and means something like " nomads " or " marauders."

THE INVASION AND THE CONQUEST

The constant unrest in Palestine, the divergent interests of the Egyptian overlord and his Canaanite vassals, created a favorable situation for the invasion of Canaan by the Hebrews, who escaped from the forced labor service of Egypt and, in their search for land, attempted to gain a foothold in the fertile land. The exact date of the Hebrew invasion is unknown. However, the date most probably falls into the second half of the thirteenth century B.C., for, as archaeology demonstrates, in this period several Canaanite cities, such as Bethel, Lachish, and Debir, were violently destroyed by siege.

The earliest mention of Israel outside the Bible also belongs to the same period. Merneptah, a Pharaoh of Egypt, erected a stone monument commemorating his triumphant campaign against Canaanite, Hittite, and Hurrian cities that apparently had challenged the Pharaoh's nominal reign over them. On this monument is a victory hymn in which Merneptah boasts that "Israel is destroyed and became seedless." Though this is a thorough exaggeration, characteristic of the court poets of the ancient Near East, it conveniently proves that some Hebrews were in the territory of Palestine around 1230 B.C. Some scholars think that the monument also demonstrates that Israel was still a nomadic people at that time. In Egyptian writing, a determinative sign is placed before names to show what kind of things they were. With the names of the settled people, the sign for "land" appears on Merneptah's monument. In contrast to this, the name "Israel" has the determinative "people," as if to indicate that the Hebrews were already in Canaan but not yet settled.

The Book of Joshua, a part of the Deuteronomic historical work, paints the invasion of Canaan by the Hebrews as one great triumphal march in three stages. In the first act, Joshua, who became the leader of the Hebrews after the death of Moses, led his people from the Transjordanian territory, which had already been conquered in the time of Moses, over the River Jordan into the hill country of central Palestine. They took and razed the Canaanite cities of Jericho and Ai. (Josh., chs. 1 to 8.) Frightened by the fate of these cities, the Gibeonites concluded an alliance with the invading forces of Joshua. (Ch. 9.) This new alliance, however, had to face an immediate trial, for a coalition of five southern cities, under the leadership of Adonizedek, king of Jerusalem, attacked the Gibeonites. This attack opened the second act of the conquest, because Israel intervened, defeated the southern kings, and swept triumphantly over the whole South. (Ch. 10.) The third act unfolded in a campaign against the North in which Joshua defeated King Jabin of Hazor and his allies, and took the cities of Galilee. (Ch. 11.) Throughout the whole conquest account, complete destruction of cities, slaughtering of captives, and burning of all kinds of spoil are the recurrent themes.

This Deuteronomic report of the conquest in the first eleven chapters of The Book of Joshua is unmistakably oversimplified. The simple sketch contained in these chapters needs the correctives to be culled from other Biblical sources and archaeological evidence. When it was written, some six hundred years after the conquest, many of the historical memories had faded away. Thus the three-act drama of the conquest that the writer conceived is incorrect, but understandably so.

To give credit to the Deuteronomic writer, it must be said that he preserved information that, indeed, contradicts his own oversimplified account of the conquest. The Book of Judges contains a list of important cities, among them Jerusalem, Megiddo, and Gezer, which were not taken by the conquerors. (Judg. 1:21, 27-33.) Further, there are reports to the effect that the tribes conquered their territories independently and not in a united effort. (Ch. 1.) Other evidence, supplied by archaeology, does not fit in with the thirteenth-century date of the conquest. The results of the excavation of Jericho, if the finds were correctly evaluated, indicate that this ancient Canaanite city was already destroyed early in the fourteenth century B.C. Similarly, the conquest of the city of Ai could hardly have been Joshua's work, because this city was in ruins during the *whole* second millennium B.C.

The account of the unrelenting massacre of the Canaanites, which is the first impression one gathers from reading The Book of Joshua (Josh. 9:24; 11:14), cannot be upheld in the light of historical criticism either. The Israelites feared the Canaanite cities, which seemed to be " fortified up to heaven " (Deut. 1:28), and they were especially in dread of the " chariots of iron " (that is, iron-plated chariots) of the Canaanite kings (Josh. 17:16). It is obvious that the Hebrews, a nomadic group, were backward both in the skill of preparing weapons and in the art of warfare. The wanton general destruction of the Canaanites was a Deuteronomic exaggeration that the Biblical sources repeatedly contradict. (See Judg. 2:20-23.) Undoubtedly many of these discrepancies may have arisen from the Deuteronomic writer's uncritical inclusion in the Biblical narrative of legendary accounts in addition to historical memories.

The conquest of the Promised Land was apparently a long and complicated process. It is not unlikely that some Hebrew tribes secured a foothold in Palestine prior to the coming of those clans which shared the great experience of the divine deliverance out of Egypt. The fact that the conquest story in Josh., chs. 1 to 11, does not mention the conquest of central Palestine, the territory of the tribes of Ephraim and Manasseh, supports this assumption. These earlier Hebrew groups probably lived as farmers and nomadic shepherds in central Canaan and maintained peaceful relations with the Canaanite cities of the area. When Joshua's land-seeking people arrived, these earlier Hebrew groups naturally welcomed their relatives.

After the powerful initial thrust of Joshua's army, the conquest slowed down, and in some cases the Hebrew clans occupied only the wastelands, avoiding the mighty strongholds of the Canaanites and remaining outside the reach of the city-states. (Judg. 1:27-33.) The Hebrew clans were not strong enough to assert themselves singlehandedly against the inhabitants of the land. But when the independent clans drew together into tribes, they demanded new territories, and, since they had grown stronger, the tribes were able to back up their demands with military power. That some of the tribes came into existence in Canaan is beyond any doubt; it is especially clear in the case of the tribes of Judah, Ephraim, and Benjamin. (These names originally designated the territories where the tribes settled.) Probably the conquest was completed only late in the period of the Judges, mainly by separate tribal military action. One such independent tribal enterprise was that of the tribe of Dan. The Danites tried to include the coastal plains west of the hill country in their own territory, but the Canaanites successfully repelled the attack, and the tribe of Dan was forced to migrate to the north to find a new "inheritance." (Judg. 1:34-36; 18:1-2.)

THE FAITH OF THE HEBREWS

The social organization of the invaders was primitive and remained essentially family centered; the families regarded themselves as members of a clan. The Biblical term " family " really means " clan "; the modern concept of " family " finds its equivalent in the Old Testament expression " father's house." The tribe was simply a loose organization of clans, and its significance became apparent only in time of war when a common danger and common interests served as motivation for united action. There was no political, military, or administrative organization above the tribal level. The ties binding the Hebrew tribes together were *religious*. They inherited the faith of the fathers, the decisive recognition that the Lord (whose name in Hebrew is Yahweh) had delivered the slaves from Egypt and was continuously concerned with the people of Israel. They remembered Moses, the first prophet of Yahwism, through whom Yahweh had made a covenant with the people at Mt. Sinai. The Hebrew tribes treasured the Ten Commandments, the charter of the Mosaic faith (Ex. 20:2-17), which required unwavering dedication and passionate devotion toward Yahweh in return for his gracious care. This faith did not allow any compromise with other cults and religions, for the foremost obligation specified in the covenant was total commitment of the individual and the whole society to the Lord. (Ch. 20:3, 5.)

THE COVENANT AT SHECHEM

Being heir to the sacred, dynamic memory of the deliverance from Egypt, the uncompromising faith of Joshua's people soon had to cope with the religious diversity of the Hebrews. For the faith of the invaders certainly differed markedly from the religion of the Hebrew clans already settled in central Palestine and from that of the smaller groups that followed the main wave of the conquest. It is quite likely that The Book of Joshua preserves the memory of that meeting at which the religious allegiance of the whole people was determined: the assembly of Shechem (Josh., ch. 24), where the covenant of Sinai was renewed. According to the tradition, Joshua put the question to the heads of the Hebrew clans as to whether they wanted to serve the gods of Egypt, the gods of the Canaanites, the gods of their forefathers who lived in Mesopotamia, or Yahweh. No compromise was possible, for the exclusive character of the faith in the Lord did not tolerate the worship of other gods.

Probably at Shechem a religious federation of the Hebrew tribes came into existence. This religious federation, sometimes called an "amphictyony," consisted of the twelve tribes of Israel who pledged themselves to worship Yahweh. Thus Israel was first a religious unity, a "church," before it was a political organization. Even the name "Israel" was a religious name, a designation of the religious confederacy of the twelve tribes. The Hebrews expressed their unity in the common worship at the central sanctuary. This sanctuary, however, was not one of the many shrines of the land that the Hebrews inherited from the Canaanites and hallowed by the legends of the patriarchs Abraham, Isaac, and Jacob. The central sanctuary of the tribes was the Ark of the Covenant, the portable sanctuary of the nomadic people of Moses.

The Ark was an empty throne on which, according to Israelite beliefs, the Lord sat invisibly. This empty divine throne was an expression of two of the main tenets of Yahwism: (1) that no likeness should represent the Lord, and (2) that the Lord alone was the king of Israel. The Ark, being a portable sanctuary, rested in several places in the land, and wherever the Ark lodged, there was the center of the religious life of the Hebrews. At one time or another the Ark was probably in Gilgal, Shechem, and unquestionably in Shiloh. The Ark retained its nomadic, migrant character even to the time of David. (II Sam. 7:6.) The Israelites gathered at the Ark at least once a year to worship the Lord, and there they brought their sacrifices. Cultic representatives of the tribes, together with the Ark priests, probably attended the Ark the year round.

THE CANAANITE INFLUENCE

Although the Israelites became the masters of considerable portions of the land, many Canaanite cities remained intact. These highly civilized cities exerted their influence upon the Hebrews. The cultural legacy of the Canaanites helped the nomadic Israelites to learn farming and to adjust themselves to the new form of life, but at the same time it endangered the purity of Israel's faith. The religion of the Canaanites was a nature religion in which the forces of nature were personified as deities. The fertility of the land was the Canaanites' main concern, and to insure fertility the practice of sacred prostitution was an established part of the Canaanite cult. Tablets found at ancient Ugarit preserve temple rituals and myths of the Canaanites and allow a conclusive evaluation of their religious ideas. Their deities were not guardians of morality and justice but acted in caprice, cruelty, and immorality.

The sophisticated civilization and religion of the Canaanites exercised an attraction upon the Hebrews. But the elaborate, immoral cult practiced in the artfully built temples and the luxury and corruption of the upper-class Canaanites undermined the faith and customs of Israel. The more the invaders adapted themselves to the agricultural economy of the older inhabitants, the more the idea spread among the people of Israel that the practice of farming required the worship of the Baals, the gods of the tillable land, for the latter seemingly secured the fertility of the ground. As a result, a new form of religion emerged, a religion in which the worshiper recognized the Lord but, in flagrant disregard of his " jealousy," served the Baals as well. Such syncretism, which is the name for this type of hybrid religion, appealed to the people and represented a constant danger to the faith of the nomadic forefathers. Through the centuries, Mosaic Yahwism fought a life-and-death battle against this mixed form of religion. Sometimes syncretistic religion became the state cult in Israel; sometimes, under the influence of the faithful believers of pure Yahwism, it went underground. But until the fall of Jerusalem in 587 B.C., fertility worship never ceased to be an alluring and popular undercurrent in the religious life of the Hebrews.

CHAPTER 3 | *"The Lord Raised Up Judges"*

WHEN the Deuteronomic writer turned to the era of the Judges, he expressed his "philosophy of history" with unmistakable clarity. To demonstrate Yahweh's Lordship over history, he sketched the pattern he perceived in the story of the Judges. (Judg. 2:11-19.) This pattern is a cycle of four stages, repeated again and again: apostasy, judgment, repentance, deliverance. In other words, (*a*) Israel in brazen apostasy turned from Yahweh to serve the Canaanite gods, the Baals and the Ashtaroth; (*b*) the Lord chastised his people by giving them over into the hands of their enemies; (*c*) under the yoke of their oppressors, the people repented and turned again to the Lord; (*d*) the Lord raised up a judge as an instrument of his deliverance. This stereotyped pattern appears in each of the stories of the individual judges. (For example, ch. 3:7-15.)

Actually the name "judge" is a misnomer, for the judges were not magistrates in a court. They were liberators, military heroes, who in time of great distress rallied an army of volunteers to rescue a harried tribe or a besieged city from the enemy's hand. These judges knew that they fulfilled a task allotted to them by God, who himself gave them enthusiasm, initiative, electrifying appeal to their own people, and an inner power that enabled them to perform feats normally beyond their grasp. The recurring sentence, " The Spirit of the Lord came upon him " (chs. 3:10; 6:34; etc.), conveys that these heroes received the gifts of leadership and superhuman courage, and they recognized that they were the instruments of God's will. Biblical scholars call these judges " charismatic leaders," for their office was the result of a divine grace (Greek, *charisma*) communicated by the Spirit of the Lord.

Besides the charismatic leaders, the Deuteronomic writer mentions some minor judges: Tola, Jair, Ibzan, Elon, and Abdon. (Ch. 10:1-5; 12:8-15.) They were probably not liberators but arbiters in disputes among the twelve tribes.

A careful study of The Book of Judges reveals that the charismatic heroes were not the national figures that the late compiler of the tradition thought them to be. Their influence on the whole was quite limited and only seldom reached beyond a coalition of two or three tribes. Indeed, some of the judges were probably contemporaries and did not follow one another like the links of a chain. The total of the years given to the judges is 410, but in reality the whole period could hardly have been more than two hundred years. Undoubtedly the writer constructed an imaginary chronology. That this was the case can be demonstrated by the Deuteronomic historian's preference for using periods of forty years, or fractions and multiples of that round number. (For example, ch. 3:8, 11, 30.)

These discrepancies do not disqualify the stories of the charismatic leaders as valuable historical sources. The stories in The Book of Judges shed light on the precarious situation of the tribes during this fateful period. To be sure, we cannot be certain of the order of events, but we can safely sketch a valid picture of the political and religious situation of Israel.

ENEMIES ROUND ABOUT

The people were hard pressed from every side. The first report speaks of King Cushan-rishathaim of Mesopotamia, who oppressed the people of Israel. But Othniel, the first charismatic leader, broke the foreign yoke. (Ch. 3:7-11.) If this report is somewhat vague, the distressing difficulties with the Canaanites are amply documented. Around the middle of the twelfth century B.C., the Canaanites subjugated most of the tribes. The exacting tributes paid to the Canaanites paralyzed the agriculture of the Israelites; "caravans ceased and travelers kept to the byways" (ch. 5:6). During this despairing agony of Israel, the prophetess Deborah arose and summoned Barak from the tribe of Naphtali to lead a Holy War for the liberation of the oppressed people. A prose narrative (ch. 4) and the so-called "Song of Deborah" (ch. 5; probably the earliest Hebrew poem of any length that has been preserved) commemorate these events. There are obvious differences between the two accounts, but the poem deserves more credit, since its tightly wrought form resisted change more easily than did the freely flowing prose account.

The tribes that followed Barak, the new charismatic leader, faced the dreaded chariots of Sisera at Taanach on the plain of Jezreel. A sudden cloudburst providentially swelled the River Kishon, the torrent flooded the plain, and the horses and chariots of Sisera bogged down in the mire and became easy prey for the attacking Israelites. This war was a Holy War in which the tribes of the federation participated. The unknown singer of the poem praised and blessed the tribes that had obeyed the call of Barak and Deborah and chided, mocked, and cursed those who did not come to fight the war of Yahweh (ch. 5:23). For the warriors perceived, in the easy victory over the awe-instilling chariotry and in the majestic march of the storm upon the battlefield, the very presence of Yahweh coming to deliver his own people. The sense of national cohesion apparent in this poem did not stem from political unity but exclusively from the common faith of the tribes in the Lord. In this connection a baffling problem must be mentioned: the name of Judah is completely absent from the list of tribes in the poem.

Some scholars assume that, since the battle at Taanach was fought in the neighborhood of Megiddo, it ended with the destruction of that ancient Canaanite stronghold. Since, according to archaeologists, Megiddo was destroyed around 1125 B.C., the battle would have taken place then. This dating, however, must remain tentative because the story does not tell of the siege or destruction of any city but merely of the routing of Sisera's army.

It would be a mistake, however, to assume that there was incessant warfare between the Canaanites and Israel. The battle of Taanach shows only one side of the coin. At other places and other times, the relationship between the Hebrews and the Canaanites was friendly — as intermarriage (ch. 8:31) and the spreading syncretism (ch. 6:25) show.

From the East also rose danger that threatened the destruction of the tribes of Israel. The kingdoms of Moab and Ammon in the Transjordanian territory made efforts to subject Israel. Eglon, a Moabite king, mustered enough power to reduce the tribes of Benjamin and Ephraim to vassalage and to occupy Jericho, the " city of palms," and Gilgal. The two tribes paid tribute for a while, but when Ehud, a Benjaminite, assassinated Eglon, they accepted Ehud's leadership and attacked the Moabites. By the clever strategy of occupying the fords of the Jordan, the Israelites cut off the routes of withdrawal from the Moabite occupation forces and annihilated them. (Ch. 3:12-30.)

On another occasion the Ammonites attempted to annex the Transjordanian territory of Gilead. This time the divinely chosen leader was a man from Gilead by the name of Jephthah. He was the son of a harlot, and when his brothers who had been born in wedlock expelled him from his father's house, Jephthah became the leader of a group of marauders. But the mounting Ammonite pressure induced the Gileadites to secure Jephthah's leadership and the military skill of his band of raiders. Jephthah drove a hard bargain and exacted a promise from the elders of Gilead that after the victory over the enemy he would become the head of Gilead. Jephthah rallied the men from the Transjordanian tribes of Manasseh and Gilead and led them against the Ammonites. During the military preparations, Jephthah made a vow to sacrifice the first person from his household whom he would meet on his return if the Lord granted him victory over the enemy. Jephthah's troops emerged victoriously from the encounter with the Ammonites. But the triumphant joy turned to woe, for upon his arrival, Jephthah was greeted by his daughter, his only child. Yet he kept his vow and sacrificed his daughter, who obediently accepted her fate. (Chs. 10:17 to 12:7.) It should be noted that human sacrifices were alien to the spirit of Yahwism; the evident awe and compassion of the writer reporting this event unmistakably reveal the uniqueness of the horrible vow.

From the East, besides the kingdoms of Ammon and Moab, the Midianites with their allies, the Amalekites, and the " people of the East " made repeated inroads into the Hebrew territories. These nomads devastated the land and seized the animals and agricultural products of the people. Against such locustlike invasions Israel seemed to be helpless. In their raids, the Midianites rode on camels that had shortly before been domesticated, and the speed of the camels ensured them superior mobility. (Ch. 6:1-6.) The judge chosen by God this time was Gideon.

To evaluate the account concerning Gideon's exploits is difficult in many ways. The curious facts that Gideon is also called Jerubbaal and that there are two pairs of Midianite leaders (the two princes, Oreb and Zeeb, and the two kings, Zebah and Zalmunna) might indicate that two legendary stories have been put together here. As the present story goes, Gideon called to arms the tribe of Manasseh and the northern tribes of Asher, Zebulon, and Naphtali. However, as the Hebrew troops neared the enemy's encampment, Gideon, upon divine command, dissolved his army and kept a mere three hundred of his warriors with him. In the dark of night this handful of men surprised the Midianite camp in the Valley of Jezreel. Blowing trumpets, smashing jars, and carrying flaming torches, the men of Gideon threw the Midianites into panic. When the Midianites fled, leaving their camp behind, Gideon called the Ephraimites to take part in the pursuit. The men of Ephraim captured and killed the two princes of Midian, Oreb and Zeeb. Gideon and his three hundred continued the chase and captured and slew the two kings, Zebah and Zalmunna. (Chs. 6 to 8.)

Around 1190 B.C., the Sea Peoples, a coalition of non-Semitic peoples, appeared on the scene of the Near East. The Sea Peoples invaded Palestine on land and sea and threatened Egypt with invasion, but Ramses III, the king of Egypt, frustrated their attack. Among these Sea Peoples were the Philistines, who came, according to the Biblical tradition (Amos 9:7), from the island of Caphtor (modern Crete). Repelled by Egypt, the Philistines settled on the sea coast of the Land of Canaan and created a federation of five cities: Ekron, Ashdod, Ashkelon, Gath, and Gaza. The Philistines (whose name, by the way, is preserved in the name "Palestine") early attempted to conquer the central hill country also. According to the Samson legends (Judg., chs. 13 to 16), which differ so markedly from the more historical accounts of the book, the people of the tribe of Dan and the Philistines lived on friendly terms occasionally (as Samson's marriage with a Philistine woman would suggest). In the light of the Samson legends, it would seem that the Danites left their central Palestinian homeland and migrated into the north under the pressure of the Philistines and not that of the Canaanites. (Ch. 1:34-36.)

THE INTERNAL SITUATION

The difficulty of Israel's situation was tragically increased by strife among the Israelite tribes themselves. The tribe of Ephraim aspired to a leading role among the Hebrew tribes, and inevitably this aspiration led to skirmish and civil war. The Ephraimites insisted upon their privilege, assumed or real, to participate and lead in important military undertakings. Thus they violently protested to Gideon for not calling them at the outset of his battle against the Midianites. On this occasion, Gideon's shrewdness averted the civil war, for he flattered the Ephraimites' tribal pride (ch. 8:1-3). A similar episode in the time of Jephthah ended in bloodshed. The proud Ephraimites, who resented Jephthah's victory over the Ammonites, crossed the Jordan and attacked Gilead. But under Jephthah's leadership, the Gileadites defeated and dispersed the Ephraimite host, and at the fords of the Jordan they slaughtered those who had escaped with their lives from the battlefield. (Ch. 12:1-6.)

Besides these outbursts of jealousy, The Book of Judges tells of a punitive expedition of the tribes against the tribe of Benjamin. (Chs. 19 and 20.) It happened that a Levite with his concubine lodged in the Benjaminite city of Gibeah for a night. During that night, men of Gibeah ravished the concubine so that she died. This wanton crime roused the conscience of the Israelites. The council of the federation demanded the lives of the culprits, but the Benjaminites were not willing to abandon their tribesmen. The council then called the tribes to begin a punishing expedition during which Gibeah and the Benjaminites were severely defeated. The tribes even destroyed the city of Jabesh-gilead, which did not obey the call to the Holy War against the Benjaminites. (Ch. 21:8-12.)

In the days of the Judges there was an attempt to introduce a tribal hereditary kingship in Israel. When Gideon delivered Manasseh, the grateful people offered him the kingship. According to the Biblical account, Gideon declined the offer with the words: " I will not rule over you, and my son will not rule over you; the Lord will rule over you " (ch. 8:23). These words vividly express Israel's faith in the Lord's exclusive Kingship. If Yahweh was king over Israel, no mere man could rightly claim the royal power. Contradicting Gideon's words, however, are the ensuing events, for after the death of Gideon, the only question that remained unanswered was: Which of Gideon's sons would inherit his father's royal power? With the help of his Shechemite kinsmen, one of the sons, Abimelech, seized the throne of Shechem and, in order to secure it, killed his own brothers. Abimelech's kingship probably also extended over the whole tribe of Manasseh. But no heir followed him on the Shechemite throne; the establishment of kingship, even on a limited tribal level, turned out to be premature. (Ch. 9.)

RELIGION, MORALS, AND LITERATURE

The essential elements of Mosaic Yahwism were transmitted by the faithful. But it became a common practice to worship the Canaanite deities as well as Yahweh; even a man like Joash, whose name meant "Yahweh is strong," besides worshiping the Lord, erected an altar to Baal and a wooden pillar for Asherah (ch. 6:25). In addition to the syncretistic effect upon the faith of Israel, the Canaanite religion, with its elaborate cult, pageantry of ritual, and impressive priesthood, started to influence the worship of Yahweh in a similar direction. In the days of the Judges, every head of a family still rightfully built his own sanctuary and appointed his own priest (ch.

17:5), or he himself offered sacrifices. Animal sacrifices and cereal offerings, together with libations, were brought in gratitude before the Lord.

The fierce morals of the nomads lost their intensity under the changed circumstances. Thus Jael's name was praised in the Song of Deborah for the slaying of Sisera (ch. 5:24-27), even though she offended against the law of hospitality, so sacred in the desert. Treachery, assassination, and cruelty were recognized ways of dealing with an enemy. The depravity of the sophisticated Canaanites perverted some of the people of Israel too. (Ch. 19:22.) But the tribal war proclaimed against the Benjamites witnesses to a cruel but healthy reaction of an uncorrupted people to a wanton crime.

The beginnings of literature in its unwritten form are certainly rooted in the nomadic times, but in the days of the Judges, literature reached a new height and brought forth admirable masterpieces. The passionate, triumphal mood of the Song of Deborah (ch. 5) and the dignified simplicity and economy of words in Jotham's fable (ch. 9:7-15) qualify them as great literature — in fact, among the most superb literary pieces of the world.

CHAPTER 4 | *" Set a King Over Us "*

For a century the power of the Philistines constantly increased. As the Samson legends indicate (Judg., chs. 13 to 16), for a time the Hebrews stood valiantly against their attacks, but about 1060 B.C. the Philistines grew strong enough to break the resistance of Israel. They invaded Ephraim. The first battle, at Aphek, ended with the defeat of the Israelites. Hoping that the presence of Yahweh would bring victory for the people, the elders of Israel sent for the Ark of Yahweh, which at that time lodged in the sanctuary of Shiloh. But the Ark did not produce the expected victory. The Philistines routed and pursued the Israelite army, and they captured the Ark of the Lord. (I Sam., ch. 4.) And as the excavations at Shiloh conclusively reveal, the city that housed the Ark was razed on this occasion.

The captured Ark brought no blessing to the Philistines. The Ark legends (chs. 5:1 to 7:2) recount miraculous happenings: the image of the Philistines' god broke, mice ravaged their fields, and tumors plagued the people. Convinced that the anger of the Lord had caused all these misfortunes, the Philistines sent the Ark back to Israel.

The Philistines used their victory to exploit the Hebrew tribes ruthlessly. The Philistine monopoly on iron was a particularly intolerable burden for the Hebrews and paralyzed their economy. Because there were no smiths among the Israelites, they were forced to buy all their farm implements from the Philistines. (Ch. 13:19-22.) Mortal danger loomed like a thundercloud over the nation; Israel was never closer to total annihilation. Some of the elders of Israel realized that in order to save the nation they should sacrifice their highly cherished tribal independence, heretofore abandoned only for the occasional Holy Wars of the tribes. They saw that an ill-organized band of peasant volunteers could not cope with the efficiency of the enemy. Therefore the elders wanted to elect an Israelite king who could command a small but proficient standing army. With such an army the king would be prepared to fend off any attack until the volunteer army could assemble. (Ch. 8:19-20.) The king himself would be the living token of national unity, besides providing military leadership.

This planned innovation, the introduction of kingship, was a matter of concern to the religious conscience of the people. Everywhere in the Near East, kingship was ordained by the gods and fitted easily into the religious ideas of the different peoples. But the situation differed markedly among the Hebrews, who regarded Yahweh as the exclusive ruler of Israel. Thus it is comprehensible that the establishment of an earthly kingship was regarded by many as a revolt and an apostasy against the Lord. The leader of this religious opposition was the prophet Samuel. Samuel had spent his childhood in the Ark sanctuary at Shiloh (chs. 1 and 2), and there, at the feet of the visible throne of the invisible God, the conviction of Yahweh's exclusive kingship had deeply penetrated his thoughts. On several occasions he asserted that the Lord considered the people's request for a king an apostasy. (Chs. 7; 8; and 12.) The Deuteronomic historian, however, also preserved another tradition, which reports that Yahweh did not oppose the election of a king. In fact, this tradition maintained that Yahweh himself, on his own initiative, commissioned Samuel to anoint the first king. (Chs. 9:1 to 10:16.)

The exact details of how the first king was chosen cannot be reconstructed, for there are three differing traditions closely interwoven in the crucial passage. (Ch. 10.) But this much is clear: Samuel, who led the religious opposition against the introduction of kingship, gave religious sanction to its actual establishment. Presumably, Samuel thought of the future king as an earthly vassal of the heavenly overlord, the Great King Yahweh, and of himself as Yahweh's messenger, who would give advice and even commands to the king in the name of God.

Saul (About 1020–1000 b.c.)

The choice for kingship fell upon Saul, a Benjaminite. Probably Saul's victory over the forces of Nahash the Ammonite at the city of Jabesh-gilead (ch. 11) impressed upon Samuel and the tribal gathering that Saul was the God-chosen leader of the nation. (Chs. 10:17-27; 12.) As the first act of his reign, Saul rallied an army and, with the assistance of his heroic son Jonathan, delivered powerful initial blows to the Philistines at Geba and Michmash. (Ch. 14.) These victories diverted the immediate danger, but the strength of the Philistines still stood essentially unharmed and menacing. (V. 52.) Saul spent his entire reign in an unceasing struggle against enemies on all sides: the Philistines from the west, the kingdoms of Edom, Moab, and Ammon from the east, and the nomadic Amalekites from the south. (Vs. 47-48.)

The Biblical tradition is not consistent about it, but sometime early in the reign of Saul an irreparable breach arose and severed the ties between Saul and Samuel. (Chs. 13:8-15; 15.) Before the war against the Amalekites, Samuel had proclaimed the ancient custom of *ḥērem,* that is, a total destruction of spoils and captives. But Saul saved some animals for sacrifice (which meant a feast for the participants of the sacrificial meal) and also permitted the captive king to live — probably with a deal in mind. When Samuel learned of this breach of the vow of sacred destruction, he himself slew the Amalekite king and rejected Saul's kingship. There was no external, noticeable change in Saul's authority despite the rejection, but Samuel's support was lost, and " the Spirit of the Lord departed from Saul, and an evil spirit from the Lord tormented him " (ch. 16:14).

When Samuel witnessed the faltering of his hopes because of Saul's disobedience, he looked for a successor, " a man after the Lord's own heart " who would obediently follow the commands of the Lord. This man was David from Bethlehem. The well-known story of David's duel with the Philistine giant Goliath (ch. 17) might be a later nonhistorical legend, especially since II Sam. 21:19 attributes the slaying of Goliath to Elhanan of Bethlehem, a man otherwise unknown. (It is not impossible, however, that Elhanan was David's original name and David merely a throne name.) Whatever the case with this story, David was victorious in the Philistine campaigns; his success gained the admiration of the people, the friendship of Jonathan, Saul's son, the hand of Michal, Saul's daughter, and the dangerous jealousy of the king himself (I Sam., ch. 18). This jealousy brought out the defects of Saul's personality, which were drawn in sharp, contrasting colors: courage and generosity mingled with an insane desire for revenge; devotion to the Lord, with superstition; rash decisions, with their painful retractions; aspiration for a nation-wide mission, together with a horizon limited to his own tribe. Carried away by this jealousy, Saul tried to kill David. (Ch. 19:9-10.) David fled the royal court to his native Judah, where he gathered a

band of raiders. (Ch. 22:1-2.) Saul pursued David even within
his own tribal territory, but David avoided the challenge and,
with admirable magnanimity, even spared Saul's life when the
latter fell into his hands. (Chs. 24; 26.)

The tenacity of Saul's chase finally forced David to offer his
services to Achish, the Philistine king of Gath. David became
Achish's mercenary, manning the Philistine outpost of Ziklag
with his raiders. In this precarious situation, David, to demonstrate his loyalty to his own people, rendered good service to
the tribe of Judah. (Ch. 27.) David was spared from fighting
against his own people when the Philistines gathered for the
decisive battle against Saul. For Achish's allies did not trust
David and his Hebrew mercenaries and sent them back to
Ziklag. (Ch. 29.) The tragic, heroic life of Saul, torn by doubts,
fears, and indecision, ended in the very same battle on Mt. Gil-
boa, and there also three of his sons, Jonathan among them,
met death. (Ch. 31.)

DAVID (ABOUT 1000–961 B.C.)

The death of Saul signaled the start of David's impressive
rise to power. First, the elders of Judah elected David as their
king, and he established his capital in the city of Hebron
(II Sam. 2:1-4). Meanwhile, Ish-bosheth, one of the surviving
sons of Saul, became king of the rest of Israel in the Transjordanian territory. Ish-bosheth was a mere puppet in the energetic hands of his granduncle Abner, the former commander
of Saul's army. Directed by petty vengeance, Abner decided
to hand over the kingdom to David, but before the completion
of his plans, Abner was slain. (Ch. 3:6-30.) However, without
the powerful leadership of Abner, the kingdom of Ish-bosheth
could scarcely be upheld, and when two of his own officers assassinated Ish-bosheth, the elders of the North offered the
throne to David. (Chs. 4:5 to 5:3.) With the manpower of the

whole of Israel at his disposal, David defeated the Philistines and limited their influence almost completely to their five major cities. (Ch. 5:17-25.)

With the political acumen of a great empire builder, David chose Jerusalem as his capital. This was a very adroit choice, for Jerusalem, never an Israelite city until David conquered it, was not a part of the tribal memories and quarrels of the previous centuries. In addition, it occupied a central geographical position in the whole land, between Judah and the northern tribes. Thus, in choosing Jerusalem as his capital, David could not be accused of favoritism to any tribe, and he thereby gave no cause for the natural jealousy of the tribes to display itself. (Vs. 6-10.) Jerusalem was called " the city of David," and it became the capital not only of the nation as a political body but also that of Israel as a religious federation when, in a majestic procession, David brought the Ark of the Lord into the city. (Ch. 6.) The ancient nomadic sanctuary thus gave a definite religious dimension to the hitherto Canaanite city.

The king fortified Jerusalem and also built a royal palace, the latter being done by masons and carpenters of Hiram, the king of Tyre, with whom David maintained friendly relations throughout his reign. The consolidation of the Davidic monarchy required several years of war with the surrounding nations, for they did not easily yield before the rising power of David. Within the course of his reign, David extended his kingdom over the Transjordanian nations of Edom, Moab, and Ammon, and over the Syrians of Damascus and Hamath. David's constant wars made it necessary to have a powerful standing army of mercenaries, which he was able to finance from the booty of raiding wars and the tribute of the subdued nations.

The empire established by David stood on shaky foundations, for there were sporadic uprisings, not merely in the tribute-paying nations, but in Israel itself. Indeed, some of the troubles started in the royal court, for David's adultery with Bathsheba and the murder of Uriah, the deceived husband, were revenged within David's own family. (Chs. 11 to 12.) Even such sordid crimes as incest and fratricide took place in the royal house. (Ch. 13.)

Absalom, one of David's sons, aspired with insatiable ambition to the throne, plotted against his father, and abetted the dissatisfaction against the reign of the aging king. Finally, Absalom led an open revolt against his father and forced him to flee from Jerusalem with a small bodyguard and a few loyal followers. (Chs. 14 to 15.) Many officers of the royal court and leaders of the northern tribes were in favor of Absalom's seizure of the throne and gladly joined the insurgents. The situation seemed hopeless for David. But in Joab he had a most proficient general, who was able to use the military skill of the royal bodyguard to best advantage. In addition, Hushai, who remained secretly loyal to David, was in the rebels' war council and gave Absalom deliberately wrong advice. When Absalom followed Hushai's tactically faulty plan, David's troops were able to vanquish the rebels. Absalom fell in the battle, and David, grieved as a father but victorious as a sovereign, re-entered the city of Jerusalem. (Chs. 16 to 19.)

Another time Sheba, a Benjaminite, launched a separatist rebellion. In this rebellion, only the tribe of Judah remained faithful to David, but again Joab's superior military experience came to David's aid, and the loyal forces crushed the rebellion. (Ch. 20.) But the question of the succession to the throne raised new difficulties. When David was already on his death-bed, his oldest surviving son, Adonijah, attempted to seize the throne and deprive his younger brother Solomon, whom David favored as his successor. But the influence of Solomon's mother, Bathsheba, and the support of Nathan the prophet and

Zadok the priest saved the throne for Solomon. (I Kings, ch. 1.)

SOLOMON (ABOUT 961–922 B.C.)

On the whole, the reign of Solomon stood under the signs of peace and opulence. Yet Solomon could not hold firmly all the Davidic conquests: at the first opportune moment, Edom and Damascus, Israel's vassals in David's days, cast off their bonds. In Israel itself, there was an abortive revolt headed by Jeroboam, a northerner, who was the royal officer in charge of Solomon's forced labor in the territory of Ephraim and Manasseh and possibly in the whole north. With these exceptions, there was rest among the Israelite tribes and the vassals of Solomon's empire. To keep the empire pacified and to deter any foreign attack upon its territories, Solomon introduced chariotry into Israel for the first time and stationed the chariots and horsemen at strategic points (ch. 10:26). (The royal stables excavated at Megiddo illustrate the Biblical account.) Solomon strove to establish his place among the great kings of the Near East. Consideration of foreign politics certainly influenced his marriage to the daughter of the Egyptian Pharaoh. Undoubtedly, political motives were present in his marriages with Sidonian, Moabite, Ammonite, Edomite, and Hittite women also. Dynastic marriages, already common in antiquity, served to strengthen the existing ties between nations.

Solomon engaged in extensive commercial enterprises, bringing unheard-of riches to Israel. With the help of Hiram, the maritime merchant-king of Tyre, he built a fleet at the port of Ezion-geber, and these ships traded with far points on the shores of the Red Sea and Indian Ocean. (Ch. 9:26-28.) Solomon controlled all the caravan routes of the western half of the Near East, and the merchants passing through had to pay tolls to the king. The kings of Arabia paid tribute to Solomon for the use of the caravan routes. Almost certainly, the famous visit of the Queen of Sheba, the ruler of a kingdom in South Arabia, included negotiations on similar business transactions of the two kingdoms. (Ch. 10:1-13.) Another lucrative royal enterprise was the trading with horses and chariots. (Vs. 26-29.) The copper refineries at Ezion-geber, which have been recently excavated, also contributed considerably to the material wealth and civilization of Israel.

Besides these mercantile enterprises, Solomon gained his revenue from the taxation of his own people. To administer the taxation, Solomon devised twelve administrative districts. Each of the officers in charge of the districts was responsible for one month of the food supply for the vastly enlarged royal court. (Ch. 4:7-19.) The administrative districts cut across the traditional tribal boundaries; apparently Solomon aimed to clear away every vestige of the ancient independence of the tribes. But he seems to have given Judah, his own tribe, preferential treatment, for it was not included among the revenue districts. It is quite understandable that bitter dissatisfaction bred among the northern tribes, which were also hard pressed by Solomon's draft of forced labor.

The use of forced labor became necessary for the widespread building projects of Solomon. As in David's time, now again the artisans of Hiram of Tyre supplied the necessary skill and technical knowledge. In Jerusalem, Solomon built a magnificent palace for himself, another for the queen, the daughter of the Pharaoh, the House of the Forest of Lebanon (so named for its cedar paneling), the Hall of Pillars, and the Hall of the Throne. Elaborate fortifications surrounded the capital and many provincial cities. (Ch. 9:15-22.) Among the latter, the fortified walls of Gezer and Megiddo were brought to light again by modern excavations. Of course, Solomon's most celebrated building project was the erection of the Jerusalem Temple.

KINGSHIP AND RELIGION

Vast changes took place in Israel during the reign of the three successive monarchs, Saul, David, and Solomon. Israel developed from a divided, harassed people into a powerful nation. The material civilization progressed in this period from a primitive agricultural form to a more advanced stage and, in the capital, even to an urban form.

The concept of kingship also went through a marked change from the time of Saul to the reign of Solomon. Saul was only slightly more than a tribal king whose authority was rooted mostly in the influence of his own family and clan, but in the days of Solomon the Israelite kingship developed according to the pattern of Near Eastern kingship into Oriental despotism. That Saul held court under a tamarisk tree and Solomon in the Hall of the Throne strikingly illustrates the changes in the picture of royal power and luxury. Saul's kingship still kept some of the marks of the charismatic leadership; that is, it was dependent on the Lord's election and inspiration. But in Solomon's time the idea of hereditary kingship had already taken deep root, at least in the South. If Samuel had envisioned the king as an earthly symbol of God's kingship, in Solomon's reign this theocratic theology, so characteristic of David's thinking (II Sam. 6:21), lost its vigor and real meaning.

Saul's and David's fervor for Yahwism passed, and Solomon's reign encouraged the growth of syncretism. Solomon's foreign wives brought their own particular cults, idols, and priests along. The presence and royal support of these alien shrines in Jerusalem hastened the intermingling of Yahwism and these pagan religions.

The Temple of Jerusalem itself was the most obvious expression of syncretism. The Temple, which was probably envisioned first as a royal chapel, was not larger than one hundred and twenty feet long and thirty feet wide. Yet it was not considered small, for the Temple, like Oriental shrines in general, was not built to shelter the worshipers; they stood outside in the Temple court, and only the officiating priests entered the Temple itself. The Temple had three rooms: a vestibule, the Temple proper with the altar, and the innermost sanctuary (the Most Holy Place), where the Ark rested in darkness. The plan and decoration of the Temple and its utensils, the cherubim, palm trees, flowers, pomegranates, and the twelve oxen supporting the "molten sea" (I Kings, chs. 6 to 7), reveal a definite influence of Canaanite temple architecture. Apparently, Solomon borrowed not only Hiram's Canaanite builders but also the plan and religious symbols of the Temple, for all these are heavy with pagan connotations.

With the growing emphasis on the cultic side of Yahwism, the priesthood's position was strengthened. When David brought the Ark of Yahweh into Jerusalem, the Ark priesthood, homeless since the destruction of Shiloh, settled in Jerusalem. It is quite possible that, because of their influence, the first words Solomon uttered in consecration of the Temple were the expression of the faith in Yahweh as Creator, as if to counterbalance the pagan atmosphere of the Temple's symbolism. (Ch. 8:12.) Later also, the Jerusalem priesthood wielded considerable influence in the fate of the religion of Israel. There is some indication that David actively participated in the elaboration of the cult in Jerusalem, especially in the organization of the cultic choirs and musicians. David himself was a musician and had the reputation for being the "sweet psalmist of Israel." (II Sam. 23:1.) Besides the Ark priests of Jerusalem, the Levites settled throughout the land and replaced the priesthood of some originally Canaanite shrines that had been adopted to the worship of the Lord.

In the days of Samuel, we find ecstatic bands of Yahwistic

prophets attached to some of the shrines of the North. The members of these so-called prophetic guilds bore the name *nabi* (prophet). Unfortunately, the Hebrew language does not· distinguish between these ecstatics and prophets of the stature of Amos, Isaiah, and Jeremiah, for they are all called *nabi*. The prophetic guilds can be compared in many ways with some modern, extreme Pentecostal sects. (I Sam. 10:5-6; 19:18-24.) These ardent devotees of the Lord did not particularly enrich the religious life of Israel, but they certainly contributed to the strength of the Yahwistic resistance to the encircling arms of paganism and secularism. But there were also men like Samuel, who was the prophet of complete obedience before the Lord, the sovereign of Israel (I Sam. 15:22-23), and Nathan the prophet, who denounced David, the crowned murderer, in the name of the Lord (II Sam. 12:1-12). Both Samuel and Nathan were precursors of the great prophets of the eighth century B.C., and their prophetic proclamations were soundly rooted in Israel's faith.

Literature flourished in the early monarchic period. David himself was a singer and poet; his dirge over Jonathan and Saul (II Sam. 1:19-27) expresses deeply felt sorrow and tender love, and that over Abner (ch. 3:33-34) honors with measured words the greatness of the hero. Solomon is also credited with the composition of songs, fables, and proverbs. Such literary interest in the royal court was the fertile soil from which literature at its best could stem forth.

Indeed, late in the reign of David or early in that of Solomon, a man who stood near to the royal court wrote the memoirs of the Davidic court, and these were later incorporated into the Deuteronomic history (II Sam., chs. 9 to 24; I Kings, chs. 1 and 2). This unknown writer wrote with an unadulterated, crystalline style, perceived the happenings of the court with the eyes of a sympathetic observer, succeeded in breathing life into his narrative, and presented the world with one of the greatest prose writings of all time.

Closely related in style to the writer of the court memoirs was the individual (or perhaps it was a school of authors) who first collected the cultic legends, myths, and sacred tradition of the people and committed them to writing. The collection of these treasures of the people's faith was not, however, a haphazard amassing of unrelated material. Actually, the Judean author viewed the past as one organic whole in which the will of the Lord found expression. His work, now called the J document of the Pentateuch, sketched the origins of Israel from the Creation to Joshua's conquest. (For a fuller discussion and criticism of the theory of the documents of the Pentateuch, see Edwin M. Good, *You Shall Be My People,* in this series.) The Creation (Gen. 2:4b-25), the undisturbed harmony of the Garden of Eden, man's rebellion, the Flood, and the building of the Tower of Babel are the main themes of the primeval history that serve as a dark background for the new beginning in Abraham. From the patriarchal stories of Abraham, Isaac, and Jacob through the miraculous deliverance at the Red Sea, and from the Sinai covenant to the conquest of the land, the Lord is the Lord of history. He is the Savior, who wants to perform his work among the nations through his chosen people. The author was a robust literary personality, who forged a massive formulation of faith in the saving will of Yahweh with his vigorous style and straightforward prose.

CHAPTER 5 | *The Two Kingdoms*

T̶HE death of Solomon (922 B.C.) sealed the end of the Davidic empire and of the united monarchy embracing the whole people of Israel. The differences between the northern tribes and Judah were obvious to any observer, and a mere trembling of the earth was enough to overthrow the fragile edifice that was the Israelite monarchy. The North, a fertile land, could boast a variety of agricultural products; vineyards, olive groves, and orchards nestled on the hillsides. In the valleys there was rich soil for the cereal grains; well-fed cattle and flocks of sheep grazed on good pasture. The South, compared with the North, was a poor territory; the semidesert of the Wilderness of Judah and considerable portions of the land were almost completely barren. Obviously, the South appeared to the North as an economic burden. In addition to these economic factors, the lack of a deep-rooted sense of unity among the tribes served as a disruptive force.

To all these inherent difficulties militating against a united monarchy, the innovations of Solomon added new and finally fatal problems. Solomon's introduction of heavy taxation, his flagrant disregard of tribal autonomy in the planning of the administrative districts, and the draft of forced labor caused a growing bitterness, especially among the northern tribes. The

49

luxury of the royal court and the splendor of the Temple of the Judean Solomon certainly provoked hostile criticism and jealousy in the North.

THE SECESSION OF THE NORTH AND ITS CONSEQUENCES

In the light of the weaknesses of Solomon's empire, it is no wonder that when Solomon died the elders of the northern tribes brought their grievances before his successor, young Rehoboam. At Shechem, the elders demanded that Rehoboam lighten their burden. The new king, however, not only refused the request of the northern tribal leaders but, with his brusque and cutting words, humiliated and antagonized the elders. The haughty, hostile attitude of Rehoboam proved the spark that kindled the inflammable emotions. The slogan of northern separatism (" What portion have we in David? "), first heard during Sheba's revolt in David's days, clamorously resounded at Shechem. The infuriated northerners stoned to death Rehoboam's taskmaster as the living symbol of their ignominious oppression. (I Kings 12:1-20.)

The chaotic revolution took definite shape when Jeroboam, the young rebel who had sought asylum in Egypt during the reign of Solomon, returned and stood at the head of the revolutionaries. Shortly thereafter (922 B.C.), having already received divine commission through the prophet Ahijah, he became king of the northern part of the former empire. This new Kingdom took the name of " Israel," while the Southern Kingdom retained the tribal name of " Judah." Thus the word " Israel " became ambiguous, for as a political designation it referred to only a part of the formerly united people, while in the religious context it remained the name of God's chosen people and embraced both Kingdoms.

In the wake of the northern secession, severe trials awaited both Judah and Israel. Shishak, the founder of a new dynasty, was a very ambitious Egyptian Pharaoh who had already maneuvered to disrupt the Israelite Kingdom during the reign of Solomon; undoubtedly with this as an ulterior motive, he gave refuge to Jeroboam. Now, in fear of Rehoboam of Judah, who was considering the use of military force against the North, Jeroboam appealed to Shishak for intervention. The Pharaoh gladly hastened to Jeroboam's aid.

In the fifth year of Rehoboam's reign (918 B.C.) the army of Shishak overran Judah and its Edomite and Philistine provinces. Rehoboam pleaded for peace and turned over the treasures of the Jerusalem Temple and the royal treasury to the Pharaoh as tribute (ch. 14:25-26). Shishak, however, did not stop within the borders of Judah but also invaded Israel and captured and sacked many cities of the North. When Shishak's army withdrew, both Kingdoms, burned, ruined, and pillaged, were too weak to retain all the territory that David had conquered. In this period Ammon secured its complete independence, but Moab continued to be, at least for a short time, the vassal of Israel. The Philistine dependency was lost, and Judah's only remaining vassal, Edom, attained a degree of autonomy.

The danger of war kept both South and North in a constant state of preparedness. The Biblical records offer a glance at the situation: it is reported that Jeroboam first fortified Shechem and established his capital there, but later, probably fearing the dangerous proximity of Judah, he moved his capital to the Transjordanian city of Penuel (ch. 12:25). But Penuel was not satisfactory as a capital. Still later, King Baasha transferred the capital to Tirzah, and from there Omri moved it to Samaria.

To preserve the existence of the Kingdom of Israel, military preparations were not sufficient. The Ark of Yahweh, the ancient sanctuary housed in the Temple of Jerusalem, exercised a powerful attraction (enhanced by the splendor of the Temple) for the devout in Israel. Pilgrims continued to come from the North to see the Temple and to sacrifice at the throne of the Lord. Jeroboam perceived that maintaining a religious unity with the South carried the seeds of disruption for his new Kingdom. To counterbalance the attraction of the Jerusalem Temple, Jeroboam allotted royal subsidy to the shrines of Dan and Bethel, giving them lavish decoration and placing golden calves (that is, statues of gilded bulls) in the sanctuaries.

The Deuteronomic historian claims that these bull images themselves were worshiped in Israel. (Vs. 28-33.) It is more probable, however, that the bull image served merely as a pedestal for Yahweh, who stood invisibly on it, a thought clearly akin to the ideas about the Ark. Whatever the underlying official theology was, the bull images proved an inducement to an intermingling of Canaanite religious ideas with Yahwism, for the bull, a symbol of strength and fertility, was also the footstool of Baal. Further, in Canaanite myths and rituals, Baal himself was poetically called a " bull," as were all the other gods of the Canaanites. The golden calves, the " sin of Jeroboam," certainly accelerated the influx of pagan elements into the faith and religious practice of Israel.

Syncretism, however, was not limited to the North. In the South a rapid deterioration of pure Yahwism also took place. The Jerusalem Temple, heavy with pagan symbols, was only the initial thrust of the invasion of the Yahwistic cult by Canaanite elements. Sacred pillars and wooden images of the Canaanite fertility goddess found shelter in the shade of the Temple. Cultic prostitution, one of the most abominable practices of the Canaanite religion, found its way into the religious life of the people. Such a state of affairs persisted in Judah during the reigns of Rehoboam and his son, Abijah (also called Abijam; 915–913 B.C.). When Asa became king in 913 B.C., he cleansed Judah of the cultic prostitution and the idols of Canaanite deities. An interesting side light is that, at the time of the reform, Maacah, the Queen Mother, sided with the partisans of syncretistic religion, and because of this Asa deprived her of the title and privileges of queen mother. (Ch. 15:1-15.)

The office of kingship retained its religious dimensions in both Kingdoms. The South accepted the hereditary kingship of the Davidic dynasty as divinely ordained, in accord with the Lord's promise to David that he would establish David's throne forever (II Sam. 7:16). The Davidic dynasty occupied the throne for over four hundred years and lent stability to the internal affairs of Judah. The situation in the North was entirely different; there dynasties changed repeatedly. Israel was torn again and again by palace revolts and civil wars; during the short existence of the Northern Kingdom (922–722 B.C.) only two dynasties could take root in Israel, those of Omri and Jehu.

Probably the idea that a special divine designation was the mark of legitimate kingship (a survival of the idea of charismatic leadership) helped the usurper seize the scepter and establish his claim against the heir to the throne. As if to set a pattern, Nadab, the son of Jeroboam, remained king for only two years (901–900 B.C.) and fell victim to the conspiracy of Baasha, who became king in his stead (900–877 B.C.). But Baasha could not make the throne secure for his son, Elah, who was killed after two years of reign (877–876 B.C.) by Zimri, one of his officers. Zimri, however, enjoyed the fruits of his treason for only seven days, for Omri, the commander of the army, defeated this revolt of subordinate officers and himself became king (876–869 B.C.). Omri's dynasty reigned through three generations: his son, Ahab (869–850 B.C.), and grandsons, Ahaziah (850–849 B.C.) and Joram (849–842 B.C.).

The first fifty years of the divided nation were marred by repeated warfare. The details of most of these wars between the kings of Judah and Israel remain unknown. The only episode recorded is from the struggle between Baasha of Israel and Asa of Judah. Baasha conquered the city of Ramah in Benjamin (near Jerusalem) and commenced fortifying it so that he could strategically control the southern capital. In despair, Asa bought the military alliance of the Syrians of Damascus with the gold and silver of the Temple and royal treasuries. When the Syrians attacked, Baasha abandoned his plans in the south and hastened to defend his own borders. Asa promptly used the building material amassed and abandoned by the Israelite king to strengthen his own border cities in Benjamin, fortifying Geba and Mizpah against the military menace of Israel. (I Kings 15:16-22.)

The initial enmity between the two Kingdoms disappeared during the reign of the Omri dynasty. It is quite probable that during that period, Judah, as a vassal, accepted the overlordship of Israel, but even if this was not the case, there was an alliance between the two Kingdoms. The kings of Israel and Judah took part in several joint military enterprises. Thus Jehoshaphat of Judah (873–849 B.C.) fought at the side of Ahab, the son of Omri, in the battle at Ramoth-gilead against the Syrians of Damascus. On another occasion, Jehoshaphat accompanied Joram, the grandson of Omri, in an expedition against Moab. When Jehoram of Judah married Athaliah, the daughter of Ahab, the marriage sealed the peaceful relationship and the military alliance of the South and North.

THE SYRIAN MENACE

Friendly relationships and military alliance between the two Kingdoms were necessities for both of them, but especially for

Israel, which stood in the way of the imperialistic expansion of the Syrians of Damascus. The Syrians had joined together into a powerful state in Solomon's time and since then had presented a growing danger for Israel.

The first inroad of the Syrians into Israel was the result of Asa's plea to Benhadad of Damascus for intervention against the Northern Kingdom. The situation reached a critical stage during the reign of the Omri dynasty when Israel's Transjordanian territory and the city of Ramoth-gilead, Syria's steppingstones to the domination of Israel, formed the center of the never-waning struggle between Syria and Israel. The Omri dynasty maintained friendly political relations, not only with Judah, but with the Phoenician cities of Tyre and Sidon, in order to secure Israel's flanks in the war against Syria. But the Syrians were occasionally able to invade even the territory west of the Jordan and, at least on one occasion, to subject Samaria itself to a long siege. The chronology of the Syrian wars cannot be established because the Deuteronomic writer is very laconic about the events, and the prophetic legends concerned with Elisha offer scarcely a clue in the indefinite references to a " king of Israel " and a " king of Judah."

It appears that Omri lost some of the Israelite cities and was forced to grant extraterritorial rights to the Syrian merchants in Samaria. Ahab, the son of Omri, defeated and captured Benhadad of Damascus on one occasion, and thus he was in a position to dictate the terms of peace: Benhadad returned the Israelite cities lost in Omri's days and rendered extraterritorial rights to Israelite merchants in Damascus. (I Kings 20:26-34.) Peace, however, never lasted long; there were wars year in and year out between Israel and Damascus.

The struggle between Israel and Syria subsided only once, and that was when the rising power of the Assyrian empire prompted the small kingdoms of Syria and Palestine to join

forces against the giant. Thus when Shalmaneser III of Assyria
(859–824 B.C.), a powerful ruler, attempted to extend his empire to the west, the small states of Syria and Palestine put
aside their hostilities to form a coalition that included, among
others, Damascus, Hamath, and Israel under the leadership of
Ahab. The armies of Shalmaneser and the coalition encountered one another at Karkor on the Orontes in Northern Syria
(853 B.C.). Shalmaneser claimed a great victory over the forces
of the coalition. But the fact that in subsequent years he repeatedly had to return to the west with his expeditions indicates that his victory was neither decisive nor significant to the
further development.

The Syrian wars weakened Israel so much that after the
death of Ahab, Ahaziah (850–849 B.C.) and Joram (849-
842 B.C.) could hardly rise in defense against the Syrians. How
serious the weakness of Israel was became apparent in the
Moabite revolt. Moab, which David had subjected to vassalage,
remained under the overlordship of the Kingdom of Israel
after the division of the Solomonic empire. Now, during the
reign of Joram of Israel, King Mesha of Moab refused to pay
tribute to Israel. Joram, with his allies Jehoshaphat of Judah
and the king of Edom, attacked Moab, but after their initial
victory, Mesha not only recovered but even defeated Israel.
(II Kings 3:4-27.) Mesha erected a monument, discovered in
the last century, telling of his victory over Israel.

The House of Omri and the Prophets

Omri and his son, Ahab, carried out a clever and ambitious
policy. Omri's founding of Samaria as his capital was comparable with David's choice of Jerusalem. Samaria was built on
a spot that was easily defensible, and, since it was a new city,
it did not arouse tribal rivalries. Omri adroitly established
commercial interchange and alliance with the merchant king-

dom of Tyre, and the marriage between Omri's son, Ahab, and Jezebel, the daughter of Ethbaal of Tyre, was a visible expression of the alliance of the royal houses.

The marriage of Ahab and Jezebel, however, had fateful consequences. Jezebel brought along, as a baleful dowry, the cult of the Tyrian Baal, Melkarth, and that of Asherah. The priests and other cultic personnel of the newly erected pagan shrines in Samaria enjoyed royal patronage. (I Kings 16:31-33.) However, it is quite certain that Ahab considered himself a true worshiper of Yahweh; his children bore names combined with the name of Yahweh, not with that of Baal. Yet the very presence of pagan shrines and the Tyrian priests of the queen called up the opposition of the faithful. The prophet Elijah led the Yahwistic opposition. The reports on Elijah bear the stamp of legendary growth, and the admiration pervading the legends veils the historical figure of the prophet. Still, Elijah's greatness emerges unmistakably from these legends.

During the reign of Ahab, Elijah announced a drought as the Lord's visitation upon Israel for the apostasy of the royal family. (Chs. 17:1; 18:18.) This disastrous drought struck the whole territory of Syria-Palestine and was remembered even in the annals of Tyre. In the closing scene of the drought, in the ordeal on Mt. Carmel, Elijah challenged the priests and prophets of the Tyrian Baal. He proposed that they prepare a sacrifice for Baal and one for the Lord without kindling the wood on the altars; whichever god, Baal or the Lord, would ignite the fire under the sacrificial animal offered to him would be recognized as the sole god of Israel. The ordeal ended with the victory of Elijah and the Yahwistic party. (Ch. 18:20-46.) Another story tells of the flight of Elijah to Mt. Horeb, and how there, at the cradle of the Mosaic covenant, Elijah encountered the Lord in the " sound of fine stillness " (" still small voice " in the conventional but inaccurate rendering) and received divine command and encouragement (ch. 19).

But the role of Elijah was not confined to his fight against the apostasy and religious indifferentism of the court and the people. Elijah also remained the champion of the ethical side of the faith of Israel, as becomes apparent in connection with the Naboth affair. (Ch. 21.) Naboth, a small farmer of Jezreel, declined to sell Ahab his property, which was adjacent to the summer palace of the king. When Queen Jezebel learned of Naboth's refusal, she trumped up a false charge and instigated a trial against him. The farmer was stoned to death, and his property was confiscated by Ahab. This flagrant breach of the covenant unleashed Elijah's prophetic wrath, and he condemned both Ahab and Jezebel and prophesied the coming judgment of the Lord. Perhaps the most eloquent tribute paid to the greatness of Elijah was that later generations told that Elijah, like Enoch of primeval times, did not die but was carried to heaven (II Kings 2:11).

Another prophet, Micaiah the son of Imlah, made an appearance in the time of Ahab. With his condemnation of Ahab, Micaiah stood alone against four hundred prophets who forecast success for the king's venture to reconquer Ramoth-gilead. The words of Micaiah show that the Lord was conceived as a heavenly sovereign with the hosts of heaven as retinue, who awaited the command of their king. The thought of Yahweh's exclusive kingship included the primitive conviction that the Lord had sent a lying spirit to the four hundred prophets to prepare the downfall of King Ahab (I Kings 22:1-28).

Besides these solitary prophets, Elisha enters the scene as one who had close connection with the prophetic guilds, the so-called " sons of the prophets." The " sons of the prophets," who made their first appearance in the days of Samuel, lived in communal settlements. They held ardently to the Yahwistic faith of the nomadic ancestors. Elisha led some of these prophetic guilds as a kind of superintendent. The admiration of the prophetic disciples for their beloved leader, Elisha, lent legendary coloring to the memories. (II Kings, chs. 2 to 8.) Nevertheless, his leadership in the prophetic guilds, his early connections with Elijah, and the fact that he gave prophetic sanction to the revolt of Jehu, which overthrew the house of Omri, are easily discernible historical facts.

In the days of Jehu or in the following generation, a writer or group of writers from the prophetic circles collected the northern traditions of the chosen people. The resulting literary work, usually called the E document, started with the call of Abraham out of Ur of the Chaldees and traced the happenings up to the reign of David. The interest of this work is clearly centered around the meaning of God's plan for his chosen people, and great prophetic personalities, such as Moses and Samuel, appear in the foreground of the writing.

THE REVOLUTION OF JEHU

In 842 B.C. the revolution of Jehu gave a sharp turn to the course of Israel's history. (Chs. 9 and 10.) Joram, the last king of the house of Omri, was still on the throne of the Northern Kingdom when a member of the prophetic guilds anointed Jehu, the commander of the army, to be king over Israel. This prophetic act of anointment gave voice to the discontent of Yahwistic opposition to the court and its syncretistic religion. Indeed, Jehu enjoyed not only the trust of the prophets' guilds but also the support of the Rechabites, members of a Yahwistic sect, who refused to adopt the ways of an agricultural society and remained nomads in order to preserve the purity of life and faith of the nomadic forefathers from any pagan influence. (See Jer. 35:2-19.)

The revolt exploded during Israel's war with Hazael of Damascus. In one of the battles, Joram, the king of Israel, was wounded and left his army to recover in Jezreel at his summer palace. Ahaziah, the king of Judah, whose mother, Athaliah, was Joram's sister, and several princes of the Davidic house came to visit the wounded king. (II Kings 9:14-16.) When Jehu, whom the army had already proclaimed king, came to Jezreel, the royal bodyguard swiftly changed allegiance. The ensuing massacre is one of the most bloodstained pages in the history of Israel. Jehu himself shot King Joram with an arrow, and his rebels killed Ahaziah, the king of Judah. The queen mother Jezebel died at the hands of her own eunuchs who, on Jehu's command, hurled her down from the window of the harem. All the offspring of Omri, together with the visiting princes of the Southern Kingdom, fell victims to the merciless massacre.

The revolt, it seems, was not merely the *coup d'état* of a power-thirsty soldier, for the standard was raised in the name of Yahweh. The " zeal of Jehu for Yahweh " was manifest in the bloody cultic reformation in which Jehu slaughtered Jezebel's Baal priests. (Chs. 9:17 to 10:36.) The revolt, which was aimed at ensuring the exclusive worship of the Lord, had also catapulted Jehu onto the throne of Israel and enabled him to establish the longest reigning dynasty of the Northern Kingdom (842–745 B.C.). The revolution of Jehu with its bloodshed was approved by the contemporary prophetic groups, but a century later the prophet Hosea saw the extermination of the Omri dynasty as a sin that rightly deserved the punishment of the Lord (Hos. 1:4).

Jehu's revolution had an unexpected aftermath in Judah. Since King Ahaziah and the princes of the Davidic dynasty met their end in the revolt, Athaliah, the daughter of Jezebel and mother of the slain Judean king, Ahaziah, was in a position to seize the scepter. She destroyed the rest of the royal family; only one of her grandsons escaped death and was hidden in the Temple. (II Kings 11:1-3.) It is an irony of history that when Jehu's revolution destroyed the house of Omri in Israel, it helped the last offspring of Omri to occupy the throne of David in Judah.

The reign of Athaliah, however, did not last long (842–837 B.C.) and was terminated by a palace revolt. Jehoiada, the priest of the Temple, anointed the child Jehoash as king with the support of the royal bodyguard. Queen Athaliah herself and the Baal priests of Jerusalem who stood under her patronage were slain. (Vs. 4–21.)

During his reign (837–800 B.C.), Jehoash reformed the financial aspects of the cult by directing the priests to give a part of their traditional income for the repair of the Temple. (Ch. 12:1-16.) Jehoash probably introduced this reform when difficulties prevented him from fulfilling his obligations as the royal patron of the Temple. Occasion for such financial straits could have arisen when Hazael, the energetic Syrian king, seized the city of Gath (which had already been in Judean hands for a long time) and threatened even Jerusalem. Jehoash was forced to buy peace from Hazael with all the gold and silver treasures of the Temple and of the royal treasury. (Vs. 17-18.)

One of the fateful consequences of Jehu's revolution was the complete isolation of Israel. The revolution had taken the life of Jezebel, the daughter of Ethbaal of Tyre, and the lives of Ahaziah of Judah and several of the Judean princes. It was no wonder that Judah and Phoenicia, allies of Israel in the bygone days of the Omri dynasty, now deeply hurt and humiliated, harbored animosity toward Israel. Without allies among the neighboring nations when the pressure of Hazael of Syria became unbearable, Jehu submitted Israel to Assyria's overlordship. In 841 B.C., Jehu paid tribute to Shalmaneser III, whose famous Black Obelisk commemorates the event. As a vassal of Assyria, Jehu received protection against the encroaching power of Syria-Damascus.

After a while, Shalmaneser gave up his plans for the conquest of Damascus; his last expedition took place in 838 B.C. In the next three decades domestic difficulties forced Assyria to relinquish her imperialistic ambitions in the west. Freed from the Assyrian danger, Hazael turned with full force against the isolated kingdom of Jehu. Indeed, during Jehu's reign, Hazael conquered the Transjordanian territories in fierce campaigns. In the course of these attacks the Syrians committed atrocities so horrifying that even a century later Amos condemned them (Amos 1:3). During the reign of Jehoahaz, the son of Jehu (815–801 B.C.), Hazael made Israel in effect a province of Syria. Now Hazael had free access to the region west of the Jordan and could lay siege to Gath and Jerusalem. (II Kings 12:17-18.)

THE INTERLUDE OF PROSPERITY

The Syrian domination of Israel ended when Adadnirari III, an ambitious and powerful ruler of Assyria, checked the might of Syria and exacted heavy tributes from it. By 802 B.C., Syria was exhausted militarily, and thus Joash (or Jehoash) of Israel (801–786 B.C.) liberated the territories that his father, Jehoahaz, had lost to Syria (ch. 13:24-25). Taking advantage of the favorable international situation, Amaziah of Judah (800–783 B.C.) reconquered Edom, which had been a Judean dependency (ch. 14:7).

Apparently under the influence of his victory over Edom, Amaziah overestimated his own military power and challenged the sister nation, Israel. The enterprise ended with Judah's defeat at Beth-shemesh, where the victorious king of Israel captured Amaziah himself. (Amaziah was apparently released from Joash later under unknown circumstances.)

Joash also besieged Jerusalem, and when the city fell he seized the Temple and the royal treasuries (vs. 8-14). Later, probably as a reaction to the bitter defeat of their army, the Judeans conspired against and slew King Amaziah. The conspirators made Amaziah's son, Uzziah (or Azariah), who was sixteen years old, king over Judah. (Vs. 19-22.)

The following decades were advantageous both for Israel and Judah. Assyria was strong enough to keep Syria in check but could not raise sufficient power to invade the territories of the two Hebrew Kingdoms. This international balance of power created a favorable atmosphere for both Kingdoms, which thus enjoyed a new prosperity under the long reigns of their kings, Jeroboam II of Israel (786–746 B.C.) and Uzziah of Judah (783–742 B.C.).

INJUSTICE AND APOSTASY

Under Jeroboam II the glory of the Northern Kingdom rose anew, for he restored the ideal borders of Israel, from Lebanon to the Dead Sea. (Vs. 23-28.) In international influence and domestic prosperity, the reign of Jeroboam II is comparable with that of Solomon. Like Solomon, Jeroboam established profitable commercial relations with Phoenicia. At this time Phoenician colonies dotted the shores and islands of much of the Mediterranean Sea; certainly, economic ties with this widespread merchant empire helped to lift the standard of material civilization in Israel and also hastened the birth of a strong merchant class. But this new Israelite merchant class, with insatiable appetite for profit, selfishly exploited the small landholders. The merchants extended credit to the small farmers with extremely high interest rates. Even with a good harvest, the farmers groaned under the heavy burden of exorbitant interest and could scarcely avoid a paralyzing impoverishment. But when the harvest failed, the small farmers lost their holdings and sometimes had to sell themselves and their families as slaves.

Thus, painful contrasts developed: the poor had hardly enough to eat, but the rich enjoyed the greatest luxury. Besides the fact that such economic injustice was a breach of Israel's covenantal obligations toward Yahweh and thus had manifest religious dimensions, there was also the specifically religious offense of apostasy in Israel. Canaanite Baalism and syncretism permeated the whole religious life of Israel, even the shrines of the Lord in Bethel and Dan being no exceptions.

Against this background of glittering luxury and naked poverty, sumptuous ritual and religious indifference, two prophets, Amos and Hosea, arose during the last years of the reign of Jeroboam II. Both prophets were called by God to raise their voices against the idle luxury, the selfish exploitation of the poor, and the misuse of power.

At the shrine of Bethel, during a joyous celebration, Amos shouted the frightening message of the coming judgment on Israel. Amos' eyes saw the imminent conflagration, and he warned: "Seek good, and not evil, that you may live; and so the Lord, the God of hosts, will be with you, as you have said. Hate evil, and love good, and establish justice in the gate." (Amos 5:14-15.) Amos transformed the popular conception of the "Day of the Lord," in which God was expected to give victory to his chosen people over all their enemies, into the Day of Judgment over Israel.

The denunciation of social injustice as a revolt against the Lord himself also appeared in the prophecy of Hosea, but Hosea went a step farther — he emphasized the apostasy of Israel. Hosea viewed the sins of social and religious life through his domestic tragedy. He saw a parallel between the adultery of his wife, Gomer, and the breach of the covenant by the people of Israel. The pathos and misery of his betrayed love for Gomer served as a vehicle for understanding and expressing the rejected love and renewed grace of the Lord (Hos., chs. 1 to 3). Therefore, Hosea called the worship of the Baals adultery. But even the cult dedicated to Yahweh was repugnant if sacrifice alone, without the steadfast love desired by God, was to be the sole response to his divine grace (ch. 6:4-6).

THE EXPANSION OF JUDAH

Meanwhile, the reign of King Uzziah brought prosperity to the Southern Kingdom where, as in Israel, a new merchant class emerged and wielded powerful influence. In Judah, however, the inequality of the social classes did not deteriorate into gross injustice as it had in Israel. Uzziah organized a well-equipped and effective army and brought the Philistine cities of Gath and Ashdod under the dominance of Judah. He fortified Jerusalem and several important places in the country. To secure the caravan routes to his seaport at Eloth (close to Solomon's port of Ezion-geber), Uzziah led military expeditions against the Ammonites and the Arabs. Through the port of Eloth, Judah traded with the kingdoms of southern Arabia. (II Chron., ch. 26.) In the last years of his reign, Uzziah, stricken with leprosy, was deprived of the public exercise of royal power, and his son, Jotham, became regent in his stead (about 750–742 B.C.). Jotham ruled as a king for only a short time (742–735 B.C.). It is an interesting sidenote that at the excavations of the port of Ezion-geber, Jotham's royal seal was unearthed.

While the long and prosperous reigns of Jeroboam II of Israel and Uzziah of Judah were coming to an end, the power of Assyria soared toward new heights. Tiglath-pileser III (Biblical " Pul ") aspired to unite the known world under the sway of Assyria. After consolidating his situation at home, in

743 B.C. Tiglath-pileser turned toward the west to bring his plans to realization. A hastily formed coalition of the small states of the Fertile Crescent (Tiglath-pileser attributed the role of leader to Uzziah) tried to halt the Assyrian conqueror. The impact of the formidable army of Tiglath-pileser, however, reduced both Syria and the Hebrew Kingdoms to tribute-paying vassals.

THE END OF THE NORTHERN KINGDOM

Besides the Assyrian menace to the existence of Israel, internal troubles aggravated the plight of the Northern Kingdom. After the death of Jeroboam II, his son Zechariah reigned for only six months (746–745 B.C.) before being murdered by Shallum, who, a month later, was slain by Menahem. With extreme cruelty Menahem broke the opposition and consolidated his reign (745–738 B.C.; II Kings 15:8-16). In 738 B.C., a new coalition of the Syrian states rose against the suzerainty of Assyria; it seems that Menahem also participated in this futile revolt. Both the annals of Tiglath-pileser and the Bible report that Menahem became the vassal of Assyria again. The heavy tribute that Menahem had to pay and the humiliating state of Israel gave ample impetus to the rise of an anti-Assyrian party in Israel. The anti-Assyrian sentiment swept away Pekahiah, the son of Menahem, after two short years of reign (738–737 B.C.). The leader of the conspiracy was Pekah, who usurped the throne in 737 B.C. and attempted to liberate Israel from the Assyrian yoke. (Vs. 17-28.)

Indeed, Pekah of Israel, together with Rezin of Damascus, formed an alliance into which they hoped to draw all the smaller states of the Syria-Palestinian region. To create a massive military bloc against Syria, the allies needed the participation of Judah, which was one of the larger nations. Ahaz (or Jehoahaz), the son of Jotham, was then reigning in Judah

(735–715 B.C.). Since he did not want to join the coalition of Israel and Syria, the allies decided to use force against Judah and to set a Syrian as king on David's throne.

In 735 B.C., Pekah of Israel and Rezin of Damascus besieged Jerusalem. Edom used this occasion to shake off the Judean yoke and captured the important port of Eloth (or Elath). In this critical hour, in spite of the message of the prophet Isaiah not to fear the allies and to place his trust in the Lord alone (Isa. 7:1-17), Ahaz sent for the help of Tiglath-pileser of Assyria (II Kings 16:1-9). Tiglath-pileser came (presumably he would have come anyway without an appeal from Ahaz), forced the surrender of Damascus, overran Israel, and occupied it, except for the territory of Ephraim and western Manasseh. The occupied territories of Israel were annexed as provinces of the Assyrian empire. Part of the Israelite population was deported into Assyria. A man named Hoshea murdered Pekah, the king of Israel, and seized his throne, but Hoshea's reign over the remains of the Israelite Kingdom (732–724 B.C.) was hardly more than colonial governorship in the name of Assyria. (Ch. 15:29-30.)

Ahaz's submission to the overlordship of Assyria deepened the syncretism in Jerusalem. Ahaz removed the old altar of the Lord from the Temple and erected instead a copy of an Assyrian altar that he had seen when he had paid homage to Tiglath-pileser in Damascus. (Ch. 16:10-20.) But Ahaz's indifference toward Israel's faith and his inclination to pagan practices bore even worse fruits. Ahaz, undoubtedly in a desperate situation, sacrificed his son as a burnt offering (v. 3); the prophet Micah, Ahaz's contemporary, probably alluded to this incident when he said: " Shall I give my first-born for my transgression, the fruit of my body for the sin of my soul? " (Micah 6:7).

The overwhelming power of Assyria could restrain the

Israelites' anti-Assyrian party but could not break it. Hoshea, the king of Israel, docilely paid tribute to Tiglath-pileser and for a while to his successor Shalmaneser V. Trusting in the promised military support of Sib'e (Biblical "So"), the "king of Egypt" ("commander in chief" according to Assyrian documents), Hoshea declined to pay further tribute to Assyria in 725 B.C. But Egypt, broken into small city-states, was not in a position to help Israel against Assyria. When the Assyrian forces came in 724 B.C., they captured Hoshea and besieged Samaria. After a siege lasting more than two years, the heroic defenders surrendered in 722 B.C. to Sargon, the general and successor to Shalmaneser. (II Kings 17:1-6.) Thus the Kingdom of Israel came to its sudden end.

Sargon made sure that Israel would not rise again. Carrying into exile the population of the conquered cities was his instrument to prevent any rebellion. In his report of the victory over Israel, Sargon tells of deporting almost thirty thousand captives from Samaria into the remotest regions of the Assyrian empire. Settled in small groups, the exiles soon lost their separate national identity and melted into the local population.

The political, religious, and cultural leaders of Israel being deported, Sargon filled their places with a newly created aristocracy. He resettled a motley group of people gathered from the far corners of the Assyrian empire in Samaria. The new inhabitants of Samaria brought along a variety of cults and gods. Thus many gods from all over the Near East were worshiped in Samaria, but this foreign population also recognized Yahweh as the god of the land. Slowly these people were assimilated into the Israelites that remained in the country, and a new nation, the Samaritans, emerged. (Vs. 24-41.)

Assyria became the supreme mistress of the Near East. In the end of Israel's national existence, the eyes of many saw only the might of the gods of Assyria overpowering the Lord and his people in the Kingdom of Israel. But prophets had proclaimed, even before the disaster occurred, that the Lord himself would judge his apostate people. Amos and Hosea conceived the Lord as King over history, who had the power to use nations in the judgment over his people Israel. Isaiah also maintained that the frightening power of Assyria in itself was nothing but an unconscious "rod of [God's] anger" (Isa. 10:5). So despite the annihilation of the Kingdom of Israel, the faith of Israel remained victorious and grew in the desperate times.

| *The Years of Grace and the Captivity*

THE destruction of the Northern Kingdom in 722 B.C. found Judah under the reign of King Ahaz, whose unhesitating acceptance of Assyria's political, cultural, and religious supremacy was obnoxious in the eyes of the faithful. But during the first half of the reign of Hezekiah, the son of Ahaz (715–687 B.C.), the international situation seemed to be favorable to the anti-Assyrian party in Judah. The yoke of Assyria was too heavy, and when the Philistine city-states of Gaza and Ashdod sensed a slackening of the Assyrian power, they refused to pay tribute to Sargon. These cities expected to obtain military support from Pharaoh Shabaka of Egypt. Apparently Shabaka encouraged the revolt of the Philistine cities, and his envoys attempted to involve Hezekiah as well. In 711 B.C., Sargon of Assyria dispatched an army under his commander in chief. The expected Egyptian backing failed, and the Assyrians swiftly defeated the rebellious cities. Hezekiah did not participate in this revolt, thanks to Isaiah's warning that Judah could not count on the help of the Egyptians (Isa., ch. 20).

Sargon crushed the revolt but could not quell the dissatisfaction of the vassals. His death in 705 B.C. seemed to be an opportune time for these vassal states to shake off the yoke of Assyria. Revolts flared up in every corner of the vast empire.

Sennacherib, the son of Sargon, had to put down these uprisings in the first years of his reign. In Mesopotamia, Merodach-baladan fought to secure the independence of Babylon and thus started this ancient kingdom on the road to resurgence.

In Palestine, King Hezekiah organized and led a coalition to which the Philistine cities of Ashkelon and Ekron also belonged. Hezekiah, looking for a broad foundation for his politics, tried to secure the assistance of Shabaka of Egypt and the alliance of Merodach-baladan of Babylon whose envoys visited Hezekiah (II Kings 20:12-19). Threatened from several directions, Sennacherib had to proceed cautiously and to attempt to subdue the rebelling subject nations one after the other. Thus it was only after he had successfully contained the troubles on his eastern flank that he was able to lead his forces against the rebels in the west.

The delay in Assyrian reaction gave Judah a breathing space in which she consolidated her newly won liberty. Hezekiah expressed Judah's independence not only in reclaiming his sovereignty but also in his religious reforms. Hezekiah destroyed all the cultic objects of the Temple that were of Assyrian origin. But in addition to these, idols, sacred pillars, and altars of the syncretistic religion were eliminated. Hezekiah even demolished an ancient Israelite emblem, the bronze serpent of Moses (II Kings 18:1-4; see Num. 21:4-9). The reform of Hezekiah was no doubt inspired by the faithful followers of Yahwism, among whom Isaiah occupied an eminent place.

The international political situation, however, degenerated quickly. After securing his throne at home in Assyria and defeating Merodach-baladan in Babylon, Sennacherib turned against the rebellious West. In 701 B.C., the Assyrian army hastened toward Palestine, and after the surrender of the city of Sidon, the Assyrian hosts did not encounter much armed opposition. Moab, Edom, and Ammon accepted anew the Assyrian vassalage. One after the other, Sennacherib captured the Philistine cities and the fortified provincial cities of Judah. This time, the Egyptians intervened under the command of Prince Tirhakah, a nephew of Shabaka, but could not stop the Assyrian onslaught. Hezekiah, who prior to the expedition of Sennacherib had fortified Jerusalem and, by building the Siloam tunnel, had assured the water supply for the time of siege, now was all alone and had to accept the terms of peace dictated by the Assyrians. He paid an extremely heavy tribute, which exhausted all the resources of the Temple and the court. Sennacherib subjected much of the territory of western Judah to the jurisdiction of those Philistine cities which had remained loyal during the revolt. At a later date, the Assyrians probably besieged Jerusalem again, but apparently a pestilence in their camp forced them to withdraw from the city. (II Kings 19:35-37.)

Sometime at the end of Hezekiah's reign or during the early part of the reign of Manasseh the old prophet Isaiah died. The keynote of Isaiah's prophecies was given in his initial vision in the Temple, in which he became acutely aware of the sovereign Kingship of the Lord. (Isa., ch. 6.) In the overwhelming light of God's holiness, the sinfulness of the nation became emphatically obvious. Pride, injustice, greed, exploitation of the poor, oppression of the defenseless, general corruption, bribery, vanity, and senseless carousing were rampant in Judah. Isaiah condemned the sacrifices, the appointed feasts, Sabbath, and the solemn assembly of the worshipers, for they became empty celebrations of a piety that was not born out by deeds. (Ch. 1:10-17.) So Isaiah proclaimed the judgment of God on the people of Judah.

Isaiah's prophecy, however, went beyond doom and recognized that divine mercy would use the "remnant," a humble and loyal core within the rebellious people of Judah, as an instrument of God's will. The prophet looked forward to the peace of God and to the just and righteous reign of a child whose name would be "Wonderful Counselor, Mighty God, Everlasting Father, Prince of Peace" (ch. 9:2-7).

After the death of Hezekiah, his son, Manasseh (687–642 B.C.), brought bitter days upon Yahweh's faithful. Manasseh accepted the overlordship of Assyria, and as a sign of his loyalty he abolished all the reforms of Hezekiah and reintroduced all the former pagan religious symbols and practices. He reinstated the high places and the worship of the Assyrian star-deities in the Temple of Jerusalem as a recognition of the Assyrian suzerainty. The Assyrians rewarded Manasseh's loyalty by entrusting him with the administration of the Judean territories that had been under Philistine jurisdiction for a while. But in Jerusalem the Yahwistic party could not accept silently the triumph of paganism. Following their protest, a reign of terror started, and "Manasseh shed very much innocent blood, till he had filled Jerusalem from one end to another" (II Kings 21:16). Nor did the situation change much during the short reign of Amon (642–640 B.C.).

JOSIAH'S REFORM

In the seventh century B.C., the Assyrian empire reached the highest summit of its power — and also its sudden fall. Esarhaddon (681–669 B.C.) of Assyria even invaded Egypt, and his successor, Ashurbanipal (669–633 B.C.), held the vast empire together with a firm grip. During the days of Ashurbanipal, Nineveh, the Assyrian capital, became a great cultural center, for Ashurbanipal had a great interest in preserving the past. He sent emissaries throughout the land to collect copies of the ancient literature of Mesopotamia for his library. Indeed, were it not for that library, which modern archaeologists have excavated and deciphered, we would know much less about the myths, legends, and history of ancient Babylon and Assyria. But, in spite of the power, splendor, and culture of Ashurbanipal's era, the days of Assyria were already numbered.

Assyria's star was declining. Yet Ashurbanipal was still able to cope with the situation when a civil war broke out. But his successors did not have sufficient strength to avert the decay. Egypt attained independence again under the reign of the native Twenty-sixth Dynasty. Babylon freed herself from the Assyrian vassalage in 625 B.C., and her ruler, Nabopolassar, laid the foundations for a new Babylonian empire. The end of Nineveh drew near as the prophet Nahum so clearly foresaw and so feverishly expected. In 612 B.C., the Babylonians, the Medes (inhabitants of the Iranian plateau), and the Scythians (nomadic tribes from the steppes of modern European Russia) united in an onslaught against Assyria. In that same year Nineveh fell, the last Assyrian king perishing in the defense of the city. Some Assyrian troops fought in the north for three more years, but they could not ward off the end. A new age, that of Babylon, opened its gates for the march of history.

The increasing weakness of Assyria following the death of Ashurbanipal was not a matter of indifference for Judah. Around 630 B.C., Josiah (640-609 B.C.) was able to reclaim the independence of his kingdom and to annex the territories of the former tribes of Manasseh and Ephraim and even Galilee. Important though these changes were, they were dwarfed by the far-reaching religious reforms of Josiah.

In 622 B.C., in the course of some repairs made in the Temple, a book of law was found. Presumably during Manasseh's persecutions, disciples of the eighth-century prophets, refugees from the northern prophetic guilds, and the loyal priests of the Temple collected and formulated the laws as admonitions and assistance for the faithful. They deposited this book of law in the Temple, and there it was found decades later.

When King Josiah read the book of law (which was the main body of the book of Deuteronomy), he realized with fear how far the religion of Judah had departed from the faith of the fathers. (II Kings, ch. 22.) For the book proclaimed that God's chosen people should have worshiped Yahweh exclusively, allowed no pagan elements in the ritual of the Temple, and declared illegitimate all the provincial shrines and high places.

The law code recognized the Temple of Jerusalem as the sole legitimate place of worship where sacrifices could be offered to the Lord. This book of law attempted to spell out in specific commandments and prohibitions the faith of Moses and the prophets. These laws were not sheer legalistic regulations, for they were animated by the commandment of love: "You shall love the Lord your God with all your heart, and with all your soul, and with all your might" (Deut. 6:5).

Josiah called for national repentance, and he and his people pledged themselves to keep faithfully the statutes of the law. The ensuing reforms were radical. First, the king purified the Temple from the cultic objects of the syncretistic Yahwism and from the idols of the Assyrian star-deities. He abolished the temple of Bethel and the provincial shrines, the high places. Josiah ordered the Yahweh priests of the provinces to come to Jerusalem and live in the shadow of the Temple. (II Kings 23:1-25.) Preachers went around in the land expounding the covenantal obligations of the people of Israel. The hope rose that Israel could and would live according to the will of the Lord. This hope also pervaded the great Deuteronomic historical work written in Josiah's days, which illustrated in the events of the past (from Joshua to Josiah) that apostasy provoked divine retribution.

The life of Josiah ended suddenly and unexpectedly in a battle against Neco, the new Pharaoh of Egypt. Neco recognized in the rise of Babylon a threat to his own power, and therefore he saw his best interest served in aiding the remnants of the Assyrian army in their desperate struggle against Babylon. He also undoubtedly wanted to conquer the region of Syria-Palestine, which had become independent when the power of Assyria declined. When in 609 B.C., Neco headed toward the Euphrates to assist the Assyrians, Josiah attacked the Egyptian army at Megiddo. Judah's destiny was at stake. The battle of Megiddo, where Josiah died, shattered the hopes of national independence, for Judah then fell into the hands of Egypt. In Jerusalem the people enthroned Jehoahaz II, the son of Josiah, but after three months Neco summoned Jehoahaz and sent him to Egypt like a criminal in chains. The people of Judah were compelled to pay a heavy tribute to the Pharaoh. Neco made Jehoiakim, another son of Josiah, vassal king over Judah. (609–598 B.C.; vs. 28-37.)

In the Hands of Babylon

The Egyptian overlordship in Palestine was a brief episode. The Babylonians, having established their empire in Mesopotamia on the ruins of Assyria, soon turned toward the west in an attempt to annex it to their new empire. Led by Nebuchadnezzar, an extremely energetic soldier, the Babylonian army faced Neco's Egyptian host at Carchemish on the Euphrates in 605 B.C. Neco's army was severely defeated, and the Egyptian aspirations to world leadership were shattered. Never again did Egypt become a great power. As for Judah, she prudently acknowledged the Babylonian suzerainty.

At first, King Jehoiakim of Judah paid tribute to Nebuchadnezzar, but after three years he rebelled. Nebuchadnezzar dispatched his western garrison together with armies from the vassal nations of the Syrians, Moabites, and Ammonites to punish Jehoiakim. When they could not break Judah, Nebuchadnezzar himself came with a great army in 598 B.C. The city of Jerusalem was besieged, and the young King Jehoiachin (his father, Jehoiakim, had died shortly before) surrendered to Nebuchadnezzar, who took him, along with the elite of the people of Judah and the craftsmen of Jerusalem, and deported them as captives into Babylon. Then Nebuchadnezzar appointed Zedekiah, a member of the royal family, as king of Judah (597-587 B.C.; ch. 24). Zedekiah's reign led to the end of Judah, for after an initial period of loyal vassalage he attempted to secure Egyptian support for a rebellion against Babylon.

In these critical times, Jeremiah proclaimed that the tragic fate of the nation was in accord with the will of the Lord, that Nebuchadnezzar executed the judgment as a servant of the Lord (Jer. 27:6). Accordingly, Judah should have humbly accepted the visitation of the Lord and should not have revolted against the well-deserved judgment. Jeremiah's attitude, of course, met serious opposition, especially when the nationalistic prophets, raising the nation's optimism to a frenzied pitch, stubbornly maintained that no evil would come upon Jerusalem. No wonder that Jeremiah was accused of defeatism and collaboration with the enemy (ch. 37:11-15)! Interestingly enough, the accusations of the princes against the prophet included the charge that his words were weakening the hands of the soldiers (ch. 38:4), but the very same accusation against the princes occurs in a contemporary letter found among the ruins of the Judean city of Lachish.

In spite of Jeremiah's repeated warnings, Zedekiah revolted against Babylon. Nebuchadnezzar's response came swiftly; in 589 B.C. he arrived with his army and besieged Jerusalem. As one of the Lachish Letters written during those days establishes, Zedekiah sent envoys to Egypt requesting the support of the Egyptians. The Egyptians actually came, and there was even a short interval when the Babylonians abandoned the siege of Jerusalem in order to meet the Egyptian challengers. Obviously a small army, the Egyptians soon withdrew and again left Judah alone. King Zedekiah, despite the urging and advice of Jeremiah, did not surrender in those critical days. Nebuchadnezzar resumed the siege, and in 587 B.C. the Babylonians breached the north wall of the city. Zedekiah, his family, and his bodyguard fled by night in the direction of the Dead Sea. The escape was discovered, and the pursuing Babylonians captured the king and his court. Nebuchadnezzar had the sons of Zedekiah killed in the sight of their father and afterward put out the eyes of King Zedekiah himself. Blinded, the last king of the line of David went in chains to Babylon. (II Kings 25:1-7.)

In 587 B.C. the city of Jerusalem was destroyed, and its walls were demolished. The Babylonians burned the Temple and carried away its treasures and vessels. The prominent members of the hierarchy and the leading military and administrative officers were executed. The inhabitants of Jerusalem were deported into Babylon; only the poorest remained to cultivate the land for the occupying forces. The Babylonian military commander appointed Gedaliah, the son of an important Judean family, as governor. But Gedaliah's governorship did not last long, for soon Ishmael, a member of the larger royal family, assassinated him and slew those Judeans who accepted the Babylonian suzerainty. But neither Ishmael nor the army chiefs, who still had fragments of the army at their disposal, could hope to master the situation. Thus the remnant of the army together with their families fled into Egypt (vs. 8-26) and forced the prophet Jeremiah and his friend Baruch to accompany them. But the old prophet did not cease to fulfill his prophetic duty even in Egypt, for there he preached against the worship of the gods among the exiles. (Jer., ch. 44.)

THE EXILE AND THE DISPERSION

The fall of Jerusalem scattered the survivors of the chosen people all over the ancient Near East. There were three deportations from Judah into Babylon, in the years 598, 587, and 581 B.C., which included altogether some forty-six hundred persons (Jer. 52:28-30). Besides the Judeans in Babylonian captivity, there were refugees in Arabia, Ammon, Moab, Edom, and Egypt.

With the fall of Jerusalem, the religious and national life lost its center. There was no king to incorporate the national unity, and there was no temple to serve as the rallying point for the religious loyalty of the Jews. According to all the laws of human history this dispersed people should have melted into the nations among which they lived and disappeared forever. But the Jews, in defiance of the laws of history, preserved a degree of their identity after their dispersion.

Those Jews who found refuge in the neighboring nations of Ammon, Moab, Edom, and the Arabic kingdoms left no clear trace. But the group that fled to Egypt became mercenaries of the Egyptians and settled in Elephantine on the southern border of Egypt. This military garrison of Jews left behind a collection of papyrus documents dating from the fifth century B.C. They built a temple at Elephantine for Yahweh, whom they regarded as the God of Heaven (that is, the chief deity), but in addition to the Lord, they also worshiped the gods Anath-bethel and Ishum-bethel. It is almost certain that the Jews of Elephantine brought this syncretism from their homeland.

The role of the Egyptian community of Jewish exiles is not

comparable in importance with that of the Babylonian captives. The first experiences in Babylon left deep scars on the deportees. (Lam. 5:1-3; Ps. 137.) But the appalling events of the first years were not repeated later as the Babylonians became more tolerant toward the Jewish captives. Though the craftsmen were probably compelled to live in the great city of Babylon itself, most of the Jews were allowed to live in agricultural settlements where they enjoyed some freedom of movement and even a kind of self-government through their own elders.

In such a settlement lived Ezekiel, a young priest who had been among the first exiles of 598 B.C. Before the final fall of Jerusalem, when the nationalistic prophets still proclaimed a speedy deliverance from the Babylonian yoke, God called Ezekiel to prophesy the judgment of the inevitable fall of Jerusalem and the destruction of the Temple by the hand of Nebuchadnezzar. When in 587 B.C. Jerusalem fell, Ezekiel's mission took a definite turn. From that time on, his task was that of a pastor to his fellow exiles, whom he encouraged with the vision of the restoration of the nation and the rebuilding of the Temple.

The influence of Ezekiel certainly contributed to the survival of the religious and national identity of the exiled Jews. Their allegiance to Yahweh found expression first of all in the observance of the Sabbath. Deprived of the Temple, at the gatherings on the Sabbath the exiles did not offer sacrifices, but prayed, sang hymns, recited, and perhaps also explained the prophetic words and events of the sacred history of the people of Israel. These Sabbath gatherings set a pattern for the worship in the later synagogues.

Yet the most important aspect of the religious survival was that the exiles brought into Babylon writings that became the very kernel of the present Old Testament. Among these writings were, no doubt, some of the oracles of the prophets, many psalms, the books of the Southern and Northern traditions concerning the origins of Israel (the J and E documents), and the Deuteronomic historical work covering the books of Deuteronomy, Joshua, Judges, Samuel, and Kings. The exiles did not, however, merely guard the religious documents of the past but also edited them and put into writing their own living tradition.

Indeed, feverish literary activity characterized the days of the exile. The Jerusalem priests added their own tradition concerning the creation of the world, the primeval history, the patriarchs, the exodus, and the conquest to the Northern and Southern traditions. The priests preserved much legal lore and cultic regulations, which appear in the book of Leviticus. The mature theology of the priests is apparent in passages like Gen., ch. 1, where the magnificent drama of Creation unfolds. Meanwhile, some group or an individual edited the great historical work of the Deuteronomist and brought it to its conclusion by reporting the fall of Jerusalem and the exilic episode (561 B.C.) of the captive King Jehoiachin's admission to the court of Babylon as a guest of the royal table (II Kings 25:27-30). This concluding report obviously served to convey a sign of hope.

THE FALL OF BABYLON

After the death of Nebuchadnezzar, the Babylonian empire reached the stage of decline. The last kings of Babylon, inept and weak, lived in the menacing shadow of the vigorous new nation of the Persians. On the Iranian plateau, Cyrus, the king of the Persians, united the Medes and the Persians in 549 B.C. Within a decade his empire had spread out over the whole of Asia Minor. The next step led to Babylon.

Nabonidus, the last king of Babylon, was an eccentric; by

neglecting the worship of Marduk, the national god of Babylon, he estranged the priesthood. Then he moved his capital into the Arabian city of Tema and left the city of Babylon to fall into disrepair. It is no wonder that when in 539 B.C. Cyrus' army defeated Nabonidus the inhabitants of Babylon greeted Cyrus as a triumphant liberator. Cyrus restored the priests to their original privileges, the religious ceremonies in honor of the deities were performed according to the proper cultic regulations, and the population of Babylon saw again the splendor and peace that they had enjoyed in the time of Nebuchadnezzar.

These momentous events were the loom on which the lives and hopes of the Jewish exiles in Babylon were woven. They must have noticed that Babylon was on its road to disaster. They must have heard reports of the rocketing rise of Cyrus the Persian. It must have seemed to some of the exiles that the time was near when God would mercifully pardon the iniquities of the past and lead his people back to their homeland.

This, at least, was the conviction of a great prophet of the exile who lived and wrote during the last years of the decaying Babylonian empire. His name is unknown, but for the sake of convenience Biblical scholars call him " Second Isaiah " because his work is now part of The Book of Isaiah (chs. 40 to 55; some scholars think that chs. 56 to 66 are also the work of Second Isaiah). This anonymous prophet was one of the greatest poets of all time; his superb style, disciplined poetic structure and vivid imagery, the elemental passion of his convictions, and the earnest depth of his themes put him into the first rank of poets. But he was more than a great poet; the prophets of Israel never before had expressed so clearly and emphasized so dynamically that there was only one God, Yahweh, and that the gods of the nations were senseless idols. He proclaimed that the Lord, creator of heaven and earth and maker of history, was not the God of Israel alone, but that he invited the whole of mankind too: " Turn to me and be saved, all the ends of the earth! For I am God, and there is no other. By myself I have sworn, from my mouth has gone forth in righteousness a word that shall not return: ' To me every knee shall bow, every tongue shall swear.' " (Ch. 45:22–23.)

Second Isaiah proclaimed that the time of servitude was passing away, for the Lord had entrusted the work of deliverance into the hands of Cyrus. The comforting words of the Lord promised the return of the exiles in a new exodus to their homeland through the miraculously blooming desert (ch. 41:18-19). Second Isaiah also spoke of a lowly and humble individual, the Suffering Servant of the Lord, who would embody the mission of Israel to bring salvation to all the nations (ch. 49:6). Later Jesus Christ conceived his own mission as the office of the Suffering Servant. (Matt. 12:15-21; Mark 10:45; and see Acts 8:26-39.) The prophecy of Second Isaiah gave hope and assurance of God's redeeming will, not only to his contemporaries, but also to all the generations to come.

And the expectations of the Second Isaiah and Ezekiel were at least partly realized, for within a year after the fall of Babylon, Cyrus issued a royal edict authorizing the return of the Jews to their homeland.

CHAPTER 7 | *The Jews During the Persian Era*

Cyrus' conquest of Babylon brought a welcome change to the situation of the subject peoples, for Cyrus introduced a new concept of empire with a well-delineated general policy toward the peoples under his authority. As if to compensate for the cruelty of oppression, the narrow cultural and religious nationalism, and the shortsighted economical exploitation of the Assyrian and Babylonian empires, the Persians granted some liberties to the nations and carefully respected the religious beliefs and cultural aspirations of their subjects. Tolerance in religious and cultural matters on the one hand and well-organized, strict, but just administration on the other helped to stabilize the Persian empire.

The astute political wisdom of the early Persian kings can be seen in their use of the languages of their subjects; all their early inscriptions were written in three languages: Persian, Elamite, and Babylonian. To be sure, the language of the top-level administration was Persian, but the provincial governments recognized other official tongues side by side with the Persian. In the southwestern part of the empire (including Palestine), Aramaic was such an official language, as it had also served as the international language of commerce and diplomacy in the time of the Assyrian and Babylonian empires (see II Kings 18:26). During the Persian era, Aramaic slowly replaced Hebrew and ultimately became the spoken language of the Jews both in and outside of Palestine.

The empire-building instinct of the Persians understood that, more than anything else, religion was the dearest treasure of the peoples. Therefore they took pains not to offend the religious sensitivity of their subjects. Such considerations motivated Cyrus' reinstatement of the Babylonian priesthood and the re-establishment of the state cult of the gods after the ill-advised religious reforms of the last Babylonian king, Nabonidus. This was not, however, an isolated case; quite to the contrary, the Persians not merely tolerated or respected, but actually supported, the religious institutions and practices of their subjects.

THE RESTORATION OF THE TEMPLE

In 538 B.C., in accord with his empire-wide policy, Cyrus permitted those Jewish exiles who so desired to return to the land of their fathers and authorized the reconstruction of the Temple in Jerusalem. Fortunately, The Book of Ezra contains a copy of the edict of Cyrus concerning the rebuilding of the Temple. (Ch. 6:3-5.) The edict specified that the Temple should stand on the same hallowed ground that Solomon's Temple had occupied and where the Jews remaining in Judah had offered their sacrifices during the Babylonian captivity. The edict further ordered the financing of the building project from public funds and the restoration to religious use of the precious vessels and other implements of the former Temple that had been in the royal treasury of Babylon since Nebuchadnezzar's days.

Cyrus entrusted the Temple treasures into the hands of Shesh-bazzar and commissioned him with the supervision of the construction. (Chs. 1:8,11; 5:14,16.) Shesh-bazzar was probably a Jew in spite of his unmistakably Babylonian name, but whether his title, " prince of Judah," identifies him as a descendant of David is highly questionable. Probably this title merely means that he was the governor of Judah appointed by the king. A group of Jewish exiles returned with Shesh-bazzar to Jerusalem, and there was also a constant trickle of repatriates during the first two decades after the fall of Babylon. Yet many Jews remained in Babylon. Jerusalem, which was in ruins, and the dilapidated provincial cities certainly did not appear desirable to the exiles who had gained a degree of security and, in many cases, considerable wealth during the years of exile.

In the time of Shesh-bazzar's governorship, the returnees laid the foundation of the Temple, but the building activities stopped soon after because of general apathy. The roots of apathy were nourished on the austere poverty of the population of Judah and on the misgivings that the task of restoration would be too much for them. The desperate economic situation reached its lowest point with a disastrous drought that completely stifled the interest in the rebuilding of the house of the Lord. (Hag. 1:10-11.) So for several years nobody was working on the Temple of Jerusalem.

In 522 B.C., the death of King Cambyses, the successor to Cyrus, ushered in a new course of events. Darius I, the legitimate heir to the Persian crown, had to contend with a pretender; during the resulting civil war, several nations of the Persian empire strove for complete independence. Though Darius soon subdued the revolts, these supported the expectations of the prophets Haggai and Zechariah that the powers of the world would be quickly destroyed and the Kingdom of God would arrive. (Hag. 2:20-23; Zech. 2:9-13.) Both Haggai and Zechariah thought that the rebuilding of the Temple was important as preparation for the coming of the Messianic Age, because the Lord would dwell among his people in the rebuilt

Temple. These two prophets regarded Zerubbabel, a prince of Davidic lineage, who was then governor of Judah, as the chosen instrument of God's coming reign. (Hag. 2:23; Zech. 4:6-10.) In obedience to the prophetic command, Zerubbabel and Joshua, the high priest, resumed the building of the Temple in 520 B.C. The construction proceeded slowly; there were delays because the Samaritans instigated distrust and hostility on the part of the Persian provincial governor. Nevertheless, in 515 B.C. the Temple was finished and dedicated to the Lord in a great festival. (Ezra 6:14-22.)

However, the completion of the Temple did not bring the Messianic Age closer. Zerubbabel, whose further fate is unknown, was not God's chosen one. Probably the royal role into which the prophets cast him and his attempts to fortify Jerusalem by rebuilding its walls made him unreliable in the eyes of the Persians. No doubt the jealousy of the Samaritans was also a contributing factor to the removal of Zerubbabel from his office as governor of Judah.

The rebuilt Temple created a natural center for the crystallization of Judah's national consciousness. Of course, due to its lack of political independence, the newly emerging nation of the Jews was and remained an essentially religious community. The development of the Jewish commonwealth along religious lines was encouraged by the Persians, who probably turned over to Joshua, the high priest, many of the administrative prerogatives of Zerubbabel, the former governor. The uniqueness of the Jerusalem Temple, envisioned in the Deuteronomic reform, now became a concrete fact. Far beyond the borders of Judah, the Temple exercised attraction for the dispersed Jews. In Judah itself, the Temple influenced the growth of hierarchy and the elaboration of the ritual. But religion escaped shallow formalism, for the growing emphasis on the ritual was counterbalanced by the prophetic teachings that

God does not need a house in which to dwell and that sacrifices become abominations in the sight of the Lord. (Isa. 66:1-4.)

NEHEMIAH AND EZRA

A lack of evidence obscures the story of the Jews in the Persian period. Even the information available in the books of Ezra and Nehemiah, the sole extensive sources for the period, is out of historical sequence. The reports on Ezra and Nehemiah and their memoirs appear in the historical work of the Chronicler, which was written shortly before the end of the fourth century B.C. Because of his remoteness from the events, the Chronicler placed Ezra's coming before that of Nehemiah. To establish the dates of the governorship of Nehemiah and the mission of Ezra is difficult, for the books of Ezra and Nehemiah refer merely to the seventh, twentieth, and thirty-second years of the reign of King Artaxerxes. But there were three Persian kings with that name: Artaxerxes I (465-424 B.C.), Artaxerxes II (404-358 B.C.), and Artaxerxes III (358-338 B.C.).

On the strength of the evidence supplied by a letter of the Jews of the Elephantine military colony in Egypt, Nehemiah's first governorship in Judah can be fixed in the years 445-433 B.C., during the reign of Artaxerxes I. Ezra's mission to Judah could hardly precede that of Nehemiah, for it is utterly unlikely that Ezra's celebrated reforms would have been so ineffectual as the religious situation at the time of Nehemiah would indicate. There are many other reasons that support the assumption that the Chronicler is mistaken and that Nehemiah came before Ezra. As for the exact date of Ezra's mission, it seems that the seventh year of Artaxerxes (Ezra 7:6-7) best refers to the reign of Artaxerxes II, and the resulting date would be 398 B.C.

Nehemiah's sojourn in Judah is reported in his memoirs (Neh. 1:1 to 7:72; 11:1-2; 12:27-43; 13:4-21), which are a treasury of sound information. Nehemiah, an offspring of the Jewish exiles in Babylon, was the cupbearer of King Artaxerxes I in the Persian capital, Susa. When he learned of the misery and the plight of Jerusalem, he was moved by love toward his people and requested that he might become the king's emissary in Jerusalem. A royal edict appointed Nehemiah to the governorship of Judah and authorized him to restore the walls of Jerusalem. On the strength of this edict, Jerusalem became the capital of the Persian province of Judah, which consequently ceased to be dependent upon Samaria. Of course this separation of Judah from the province of Samaria was offensive to Sanballat, the Governor of Samaria, who therefore wanted to frustrate the plans of Nehemiah. (Chs. 1 to 3.)

Thus when Nehemiah commenced building the city walls with the enthusiastic participation of the population, Sanballat and his allies (Tobiah, the governor of Ammon, some Arabic groups, and the Ashdodites) prepared for a surprise attack upon Jerusalem. Rumors of Sanballat's secret plans somehow reached Nehemiah, who created a state of constant preparedness, and the volunteer workers built the walls with sword in one hand and trowel in the other. When Sanballat realized that he could not take Jerusalem by surprise, he attempted to lure Nehemiah outside of the city by a ruse. But Nehemiah did not walk into the trap. Sanballat also accused Nehemiah of rebellious intentions against Persia and of conspiracy to become the king of Judah. But all these maneuverings did not affect Nehemiah's singleminded determination to complete the rebuilding of the city walls. (Chs. 4 and 6.)

Nehemiah's crew of builders raised the walls, as the Biblical report goes, in fifty-two days. It is more likely, however, that this surprisingly short time was sufficient only to fill the gaps in the wall and that the work was completed at the end of two years and four months (as Josephus, the Jewish historian of the first century A.D., reports). But even when the city walls were raised, the city itself was half in ruins, and its population was small. To remedy this situation, Nehemiah ordered the repopulation of Jerusalem by relocating one tenth of the population of the province of Judah. (Ch. 11:1-2.)

Nehemiah also faced other difficulties. The poor farmers were the easy prey of the rich grain merchants. In time of poor harvest or of the crop's complete failure, the farmers mortgaged their land and the crop of the following year to the merchants for food with which to exist. But the merchants charged so high an interest rate that the farmers had to sell their children to the rich as slaves. To lighten the burden of the exploited, Nehemiah offered the loan of money and grain without interest to the farmers and forced the rich merchants to abolish interest and to return mortgaged lands to their original owners. (Ch. 5.)

To enforce the observance of the Sabbath, Nehemiah closed the city gates of Jerusalem for the whole day so that neither the farmers nor the merchants could bring their wares to market. After his first governorship, Nehemiah returned to the court of King Artaxerxes, but sometime later he came back to Jerusalem, probably as governor again. During Nehemiah's absence from Judah, Eliashib, the high priest, gave a chamber in the courts of the Temple to Tobiah, the governor of Ammon (who was a believer in the Lord as his name indicates). Upon his return, Nehemiah threw Tobiah's belongings from the Temple courts and gave back the room to its original cultic use. Nehemiah also enforced the delivery of the tithe due the priests of the Temple. (Ch. 13:4-21.) In the light of his memoirs, Nehemiah appears as a devoted servant of the Lord, who understood the cultic aspects as well as the social and ethical obligations inherent to the covenantal faith of Israel. Though Nehemiah contributed greatly to the restoration of the nation, the main share in the restoration was the work of Ezra.

Ezra, a Jewish priest in Babylon, obtained a commission from King Artaxerxes II to proclaim the law of the Lord in the province " Beyond the River," that is, in Syria-Palestine. The copy of the commissioning document is included in The Book of Ezra. (Ch. 7:12-26.) There, Ezra is called " the scribe of the law of the God of heaven." This title does not imply that Ezra was the author of the law or that he was a scholar in the matters of the law of the Lord. The word " scribe " means simply an " officer," and thus Ezra's title should be understood as " the officer for the affairs of the law of the God of heaven."

Apparently, the Jews of the Dispersion had great influence in the Persian court and could move the king to trust Ezra with the introduction and enforcement of the law of God. The royal edict authorizd Ezra to cover the needs of the Temple of Jerusalem from the royal treasury, to award tax exemption to the cultic personnel of the Temple, to make collections, and to recruit voluntary repatriates among the Jews of Babylon. Indeed, Ezra came to Jerusalem with a caravan of repatriates bearing gifts from the Babylonian Jews.

As the Chronicler reports, the first problem that Ezra had to face was the mixed marriages. (Chs. 9 and 10.) Even during the governorship of Nehemiah, marriages with foreign women were a grave problem; sometimes the children of foreign women did not even speak the language of their Jewish fathers and consequently also followed the pagan ways of their mothers. (Neh., 13:23-27.) Ezra ordered the Jews to divorce their foreign wives and send them away along with their children. The cruelty of this measure cannot be excused, even though the underlying intention was to keep the faith of the Jews pure of pagan influence. But the fear of the contamination of the faith was intermingled with a hatred of foreigners. There were, however, voices that protested against this bigoted religious nationalism, and the books of Ruth and Jonah are the literary fruits of this opposition. The Book of Ruth, a superbly written story, reminded the readers that Ruth, the great-grand-mother of the venerated King David, was also a foreign woman from Moab. The other book, Jonah, emphasized that God was merciful to those who repented, even though they might be foreigners like the inhabitants of Nineveh, the capital of the hated Assyria.

Ezra's main task was the proclamation of the " law of the God of heaven." On New Year's Day, Ezra assembled the people and read the law before them from early morning until midday. It seems that the reading of the law was a part of the solemn renewal of the covenant and was completed by the people's oath to obey the law. (Ch. 8.) Unfortunately, there is no definite clue to identify the law proclaimed by Ezra. Probably he read selected portions from the legal material of the priestly edition of the Pentateuch. Not unlikely the so-called " Holiness Code " (Lev., chs. 17 to 26) formed the central core of the law read before the people. What exactly was the law of Ezra and what portions were read are questions that remain without conclusive answer. But this much is beyond any doubt: the law constituted and identified the Jews, not as a political body, but as the religious community of the people of God. The Law became the center of the cultic-religious commonwealth of the Jews.

The work of Ezra contributed vastly to the survival of the Jewish people and gave the first impetus to the formulation of the emerging Judaism. After the time of Ezra, the law oc-cupied a central, normative position in Judaism, and its regulations pervaded the whole lives of the Jews. Later the psalmist rightly said concerning the pious Jew: " His delight is in the law of the Lord, and on his law he meditates day and night." (Ps. 1:2.)

FROM EZRA TO ALEXANDER THE GREAT

Of the two centuries of Persian reign over Judah we know less than of any period in the history of Israel. With the exception of the events already discussed, neither the Bible nor secular literature, nor archaeological finds yield enough data to reconstruct the story of this period. Yet some trends are clearly perceivable, for the mission of Ezra had affected the development of the cult on the one hand and of the sacred writings on the other.

The restored Temple became the unique institution of the religious community. Unlike the pre-exilic Temple, the second Temple was no royal sanctuary, but belonged to the whole people of the covenant. The uniqueness of the Jerusalem Temple brought into being the hierarchical division of the priesthood; the high priestly office that emerged in this period was vested exclusively in the Zadokites, the officiating priesthood of Jerusalem. The Levites, the former priesthood of Israel, became cultic attendants: temple singers, porters, and doorkeepers. The ritual developed into an elaborate and solemn pageantry in which the role of the priests became paramount. The spontaneity of the worship of the ancient days, the " rejoicing before Yahweh," was all but lost in the well-organized cult.

With the centralization of the religious observance in the Temple, the ordinary laymen, especially the country laymen, lost the intimate experience of some aspects of worship, notably the sacrifices, offerings, purifications, and atonement for sin. But the religious life found a new channel in the synagogue worship, which had had its beginnings during the days of the exile. When, during the fourth century B.C., the books of the Torah (that is, Genesis, Exodus, Leviticus, Numbers, and Deuteronomy) attained a normative influence upon the religious beliefs and practices of the Jews, these books were read and interpreted, not by a priestly class, but by trained laymen. No doubt the synagogue's main purpose was religious instruction rather than worship, but the two went hand in hand. (The synagogue pattern of instructive worship found its continuation later in Christian worship.) Besides the law, the words of the prophets were read at the gatherings in the synagogues. Indeed, the formation of the Old Testament received noteworthy impetus from the synagogues of the Persian period.

The emphatic interest in the cult pervades the historical work of the Chronicler (I and II Chronicles, Ezra, and Nehemiah), which was written about 300 B.C. A preoccupation with the cult is also noticeable in the prophecy of Joel, when he bewails that, because of the disastrous drought and plague of locusts, " the cereal offering and the drink offering are cut off from the house of the Lord " (Joel 1:9). But Joel also expressed the hope that the imminent Day of the Lord, a universal judgment day, would bring the outpouring of the Spirit. (Ch. 2.) The expectation of the coming of God's judgment belonged to the prophetic hopes of the time, as the anonymous prophecies attached to The Book of Isaiah illustrate. (Chs. 19; 23; and 24 to 27.)

To sketch in detail the external history of the Jewish commonwealth during the Persian period is impossible because of the scarcity of available data. This much is clear: the Persians granted autonomy in religious and internal administrative matters to the Jews. As the Jewish coins of the period, which bear the inscription " Judah," indicate, Judah was established as a province directly under the crown. The high priest occupied an important political position as the head of the Jewish people at the side of the Persian governor. Presumably this was the situation until Alexander the Great invaded the East in 333 B.C., and Judah fell into the hands of the competing Hellenistic kingdoms of Egypt and Syria, heirs to the eastern half of Alexander's empire.

The story of Israel, so dark with misery, apostasy, and tears and so shining with hope, devotion, and faith, was not finished with the coming of Alexander the Great. A new chapter opened. In that new chapter, Jesus Christ fulfilled the mission of Israel by becoming the light for the nations and the blessing for all the families of the earth. And in Christ, a New Israel, though a nation no longer, was constituted from all those who accepted him as their Lord and Savior.

Important Dates in the Story of Israel

Joshua's people invade Canaan	about 1250 B.C.
Saul	about 1020–1000 B.C.
David	**about 1000–961 B.C.**
Solomon	about 961–922 B.C.
Division of the Hebrew Kingdom	**about 922 B.C.**
Omri of Israel	about 876–869 B.C.
Ahab of Israel	about 869–850 B.C.
Jehu's revolt	**about 842 B.C.**
Jeroboam II of Israel	about 786–746 B.C.
Uzziah of Judah	about 783–742 B.C.
Syro-Ephraimite war	about 735 B.C.
Fall of Samaria; end of the Kingdom of Israel	**about 722 B.C.**
Hezekiah	about 715–687 B.C.
Josiah	about 640–609 B.C.
The Book of the Law found; Josiah's reform	**about 622 B.C.**
Fall of Nineveh; end of Assyria	**612 B.C.**
Babylon defeats Egypt at Carchemish	605 B.C.
Deportation of the first captives to Babylon	598 B.C.
Fall of Jerusalem; second deportation to Babylon	**587 B.C.**
Fall of Babylon to the Persians	539 B.C.
Cyrus' edict permits the return of the Jews	**538 B.C.**
Dedication of the second Temple of Jerusalem	515 B.C.
Nehemiah's governorship	445–433 B.C.
Ezra's mission	398 B.C.?
Alexander the Great invades the Orient	**333 B.C.**